Ghosts of England:
on a Medium's Vacation

Rob Gutro

Cover Photo

The cover photo was taken during a tour of the catacombs in Edinburgh, Scotland in 2013. The blurring of the image was unintentional, but I thought it added visual interest, almost as if the people pictured were fleeing from an encounter with a ghost.

The experiences in this book are true. However, some names have been altered or abbreviated to protect the privacy of the individual providing the story.

"Ghosts of England on a Medium's Vacation" by Rob Gutro. ISBN-13: 978-1985276574 and ISBN-10: 1985276577.

Dedication

This book is dedicated to several people who made my trips to the United Kingdom special.

To my friends Anne Marie and Simon Clarke from Across the Pond Vacations who arranged the most amazing tours of England. A special thanks is extended to Anne Marie Clarke for her edits while working on this book.

To Paul and Sonja Fogg, owners of the Langdon House Bed and Breakfast, who made us feel at home while being away from home.

To my husband and silent partner Tom for his edits and help with the Tudor history in this book and for his continued support, patience, and faith in me, which made this project possible.

Contents

Preface

This book is divided into ten parts: Part 1 discusses the basics differences between ghosts and spirits; Parts 2 through 10 are organized around my personal encounters.

My previous books include *Ghosts and Spirits: Insights from a Medium*, *Lessons Learned from Talking to the Dead*, *Pets and the Afterlife*, and *Pets and the Afterlife 2*.

If you have any questions, please contact me:

Blog:
http://ghostsandspiritsinsights.blogspot.com/
www.robgutro.com or www.petspirits.com

Facebook:
https://www.facebook.com/ghostsandspirits.insightsfromamedium
https://www.facebook.com/RobGutroAuthorMedium

Twitter:
https://twitter.com/GhostMediumBook

Amazon Author Page:
www.amazon.com/author/robgutro

YouTube:
https://plus.google.com/collection/ok7wh

Email:
Rgutro@gmail.com

Introduction

When I was a teenager, I realized I had the ability to communicate with people who have passed. As my abilities as a medium matured. I also developed the ability to communicate with the spirits of pets, specifically dogs and cats. I am also a scientist, a meteorologist to be specific, and as such I regularly employ the Scientific Method to form theories and separate true paranormal experiences from what can be dismissed by a plausible explanation as normal.

What happens when a medium goes on vacation? Can a medium simply switch off their ability at will? Well…not exactly.

In this book, you will read about my experiences on two separate trips to the United Kingdom. England's rich history and many epic battles have caused an over-abundance of residual emotional energy. Everywhere I traveled, I had a paranormal experience. I explored royal palaces and spent the night in a haunted castle. I encountered the ghosts of historical figures including a queen, a prince, and a nobleman; several ghosts even shared their pain of death experience with me. On one occasion, the doppelganger of a loved one provided directions when I became lost while driving in the countryside due to a malfunctioning GPS. But not all of my encounters were of the human variety: there was also a very special visit from a canine ghost.

This book is intended to be more than just a collection of personal ghost stories. In addition to relating my ghostly encounters, I have also included a short narrative history of the place where the experience occurred. After all, knowing the history of a place is key to understanding why a ghost has decided to stay behind.

So, join me as I relate to you my encounters with the ghosts of England.

Rob Gutro

PART 1: GHOSTLY BASICS

Chapter 1:
What Happens After Death?

In order to understand the ghosts I encountered in England it's important to know who they are, or were in the physical world and why they chose to remain behind.

If you've read my other books, you know what a ghost is, what a spirit is, and what happens after our physical bodies die. However, if you haven't read any of the previous books, I'll reiterate or just give you a refresher. It's important to know the difference and similarities between them and understand why most Earth-bound ghosts choose to stay behind.

First, you need not believe in a religion to understand there is an afterlife. All you need is to understand the science of energy, because that's what we become after our physical bodies die.

"Soul 101"
We need to understand what happens to our "soul" after our physical bodies die. So, let's define "soul."

In many societies and religions it is the immortal essence of a living thing. A soul is actually the energy in *every living thing* that combines memories, personalities and knowledge. So animals have souls? Of course. Every living thing has a soul. To think otherwise is ridiculous.

Of course animals (and dinosaurs) lived and died on Earth long before humans ever showed up. They survived because they had intelligence, instinct, emotions, memories, and their own personalities. After all, what makes one animal a pack leader and not all of them? Why are some animals shy? Easily frightened? Bold? Challenging? That's personality. They all have one, just as humans do.

Animals lived eons before mankind ever walked the Earth and they would never have survived if they couldn't think, feel and learn. Every living thing has a soul.

We Are Energetic
Energy is the foundation of the paranormal. As a scientist, my focus is on energy so we'll start with the basics and I'll explain how that energy becomes either a ghost or spirit.

So where does that energy come from when we're alive? Our bodies contain energy in liquid, solid and gaseous states (even though some people are "more gassy" than others!).

Our body needs energy to work. Food is that energy. When we eat, the food powers everything. When our physical body stops working and dies, the energy stored up has to go somewhere. Stored energy is called potential energy. Potential energy is the energy stored in an object (like a physical body). It can also be seen as residual energy - that is, remaining energy leftover after most of it has gone.

Our thoughts are also energy and can be measured as brainwaves. Brainwaves are produced by synchronized electrical pulses from bunches of neurons that communicate with each other.

According to the Massachusetts Institute of Technology, the human brain contains about 100 billion neurons or nerve cells. A neuron is a cell that is excited electrically and processes and transmits information through electrical and chemical signals through the body. Those neurons are networked through our bodies, so we have electrical signals moving through our bodies.

Electroencephalography or EEG is the science of recording of electrical activity along the human scalp. EEGs measure the changes in voltage that result from the flow of electrical signals within the neurons of the brain. Brainwave speed is measured in Hertz (cycles per second) and they are classified as slow, moderate, and fast waves.

So when our physical bodies die, that energy needs to go somewhere.

That's where a couple of laws of physics come into play. The Law of Conservation of Energy was discovered by Julius Robert Mayer in 1842. Basically, it said energy cannot be destroyed only transformed. For instance, chemical energy can be converted to kinetic energy when dynamite explodes.

The law also states that no system without an external energy supply can deliver an unlimited amount of energy to its surroundings. That means that ghosts and spirits need to draw on other energies, physical or emotional energies to get strong enough to communicate, move things, make noises, etc.

I often describe a ghost or spirit as a lightbulb that doesn't light up until there's physical energy or emotional energy available to siphon. Only then can entities 'light up" and communicate.

Just a little more science to make it clear how it all works: when you couple the Law of Conservation of Energy with Albert Einstein's famous equation: energy (E) equals mass (M) times a constant squared. Basically, mass and energy are related. On the rare occasion when mass is converted totally into energy, the equation determines how much energy that will be.

Those two laws were merged into the Law of Conservation of Mass-Energy. That law basically says that the total amount of mass and energy in the universe is constant. If it's constant, then the energy needs to go somewhere or something has to change. Therefore, the energies in our bodies couple with our memories and personalities and become an earthbound ghost or spirit once they make the choice of location.

Where Does Energy Go?
When our physical bodies cease working the energies left over combine with our personalities and memories as an entity of energy.

According to the Massachusetts Institute of Technology, the human brain contains about 100 billion neurons or nerve cells. A neuron is a cell that is excited electrically and processes and transmits information through electrical and chemical signals through the body. Those neurons are networked through our bodies, so we have electrical signals moving through our bodies.

Electroencephalography or EEG is the science of recording of electrical activity along the human scalp. EEGs measure the changes in voltage that result from the flow of electrical signals within the neurons of the brain. Brainwave speed is measured in Hertz (cycles per second) and they are classified as slow, moderate, and fast waves.

So when our physical bodies die, that energy needs to go somewhere.

That's where a couple of laws of physics come into play. The Law of Conservation of Energy was discovered by Julius Robert Mayer in 1842. Basically, it said energy cannot be destroyed only transformed. For instance, chemical energy can be converted to kinetic energy when dynamite explodes.

The law also states that no system without an external energy supply can deliver an unlimited amount of energy to its surroundings. That means that ghosts and spirits need to draw on other energies, physical or emotional energies to get strong enough to communicate, move things, make noises, etc.

I often describe a ghost or spirit as a lightbulb that doesn't light up until there's physical energy or emotional energy available to siphon. Only then can entities 'light up" and communicate.

Just a little more science to make it clear how it all works: when you couple the Law of Conservation of Energy with Albert Einstein's famous equation: energy (E) equals mass (M) times a constant squared. Basically, mass and energy are related. On the rare occasion when mass is converted totally into energy, the equation determines how much energy that will be.

Those two laws were merged into the Law of Conservation of Mass-Energy. That law basically says that the total amount of mass and energy in the universe is constant. If it's constant, then the energy needs to go somewhere or something has to change. Therefore, the energies in our bodies couple with our memories and personalities and become an earthbound ghost or spirit once they make the choice of location.

Where Does Energy Go?
When our physical bodies cease working the energies left over combine with our personalities and memories as an entity of energy.

(Photo: The water in the Ancient Roman Baths, in Bath, England, provided energy for ghostly activity there. Credit: R. Gutro)

Ghosts and spirits are both beings of energy. The differences lie in location and uses of energies. In the next chapter I'll talk about what a ghost is, and about some of the power sources ghosts use to communicate with the living.

Chapter 2:
What is a Ghost? A Spirit?

Ghosts are earth-bound entities that either choose to stay here on Earth or they get stuck here. Spirits are the same entity who has chosen to move on to "the other side" or into the light.

In this chapter, I'll explain why some ghosts stay, things to keep in mind about ghosts, energy sources, how they can appear and about dark entities. I'll also explain the basics about spirits and how their energy sources are both similar and different from a ghost's energy sources.

Once the physical body dies and the consciousness awakens in the afterlife we have a choice to stay behind on Earth, as what I call a "ghost" or we cross over into the light and join the energies of the universe (Heaven/Paradise/Valhalla/Elysium) as what I call a "spirit."

Where Ghosts Are Found
The first rule of thumb is that ghosts usually linger in a place that they were familiar with in life or they linger where they died, as in a home, battlefield, car accident, or hospital. In terms of this book of my encounters in England, ghosts were found in castles, churches, villages or battlefields.

Accidents, Murder Victims
Whenever someone dies in an accident or is murdered, they may be confused when they awaken as energy. Initially, they may not realize their physical

body is dead, so they linger on Earth at the location of their death trying to grasp what has happened. Or they may find themselves in their home unable to understand why their loved ones can't see or hear them. Eventually, most accident and murder victims do realize they're dead. That's because they don't get responses from the living. As a result they cross over in a short time.

So when does a ghost get "stuck" on Earth? It seems that the longer a ghost lingers on Earth, the more apt they are to forget how to cross over. That's where paranormal teams come in and help Earth-bound ghosts become spirits and join their loved ones on the other side.

Unfinished Business
There are many reasons people choose to stay behind as a ghost. Some may have unfinished business on Earth, such as obtaining forgiveness for their bad behavior toward others when they were alive. Of course, as a ghost it's much harder for them to get that forgiveness, since most of the living are unaware of the signs from ghosts.

Religious Fear
As a paranormal investigator I've encountered a number of people who have actually chosen to remain behind as a ghost. When our physical bodies die we gain an awareness of any misdeeds we have done during our time in the physical. As a result, some earthbound ghosts were afraid to cross over because of something they did in their past. Others may think they're still worthy of going forth, but remain behind hoping to secure forgiveness from others before moving on.

Ghosts have told me because of any of their misdeeds during their life on Earth, their religion has taught them that they are a bad person and are undeserving of paradise/heaven/Valhalla, etc. That line of thought is responsible for many people choosing to stay behind as ghosts.

Remember that ghosts rarely have interaction with the living and are almost never heard and helped. So, choosing to be a ghost instead of a spirit ensures an afterlife of misery and loneliness. All souls deserve to join the energies that flow through the universe and go to whatever you call your version of heaven.

There's an important lesson here for those living and left behind. If you think someone who passed is waiting for forgiveness to cross over, then try to find it in your heart. I know that some people I've spoken with have been physically, sexually or mentally abused - and those things are difficult to forgive.

You can forgive, but that doesn't mean you don't have to forget. By forgiving, you may enable that tortured earthbound ghost a chance for peace and reconciliation in the afterlife.

Five Things to Keep in Mind
Think about what being a ghost feels like. First, remember that they were all people or animals. So they need to be addressed and treated with respect as if they were still living, breathing people or pets.

Second, to go into a place known to have a ghost and to try to get the entity to touch, shove or hurt you is the same as asking that of a living and invisible person. To provoke a frightened animal or person would only lead to bad consequences for you. I tell people who have a ghost in their home to think of the entity as an invisible roommate.

Third, treat all ghosts with respect and remember that they maintain their personalities. So, if they were nasty in life, they're likely nasty in death. If they were funny or nice in life, they will be the same in the afterlife.

Fourth, ghosts that stay longer get stuck earthbound and although they may be able to see their relatives and friends in spirit, they can't communicate with them.

Fifth, think of being a ghost as living an eternity in the afterlife in an isolation prison cell where no one can hear you. No one can let you out, either, until someone opens the light for the ghost and helps them cross over (which is where paranormal investigators and mediums come in).

To me, being an Earth-bound ghost is being sentenced to a hell. Think about that - how would you feel if you saw your parents in spirit and couldn't talk with them for eternity?

One of the most popular digital recorded pleas from ghosts is "help me!" They want help crossing over and getting out of their eternal Earth-bound prison.

So, ghosts need someone, like a medium, to tell them how to move on and open the light to make that happen.

*(Photo: Thornbury Castle, Exterior.
Credit: R. Gutro)*

Physical Energies, Ghosts and Spirits

Energy is the foundation of the afterlife. There are physical energies and emotional energies and Earth-bound ghosts and spirits who have crossed over each use both types, but there are differences.

Physical energies are used by both ghosts and spirits. Those include heat, light, water, movement and electricity. Both entities can absorb those energies to empower themselves enough to make their presence known. Think of it as draining a battery to power a flashlight. That's what ghosts do during paranormal investigations. Once a battery is drained, that's usually when paranormal investigators either hear something or feel something from a ghost.

Ghosts and Emotional Energy

I've learned that ghosts use negative emotional energy to power themselves and spirits use positive emotional energy.

Negative emotional energies include fear, anger, depression and anxiety. That's why if you suspect a dwelling is haunted and you enter it feeling anxious or nervous, you're giving the ghost a "battery" in which to draw emotional energy from you.

The most important point about having a ghost nearby is that although they absorb negative emotional energy, they also emit it. Having a ghost in your house will cause disruption to the living on an emotional scale. Ghosts emit negative energy which leads to disagreements, arguments and bad feelings among the living, which is why they need to go into the light. If you can't get them to move on by telling them to go on, then you need to contact a paranormal group to help cross them over.

Crossing a ghost over means a ghost becomes a spirit and is free of its bonds to Earth. Spirits are the same energy entities, but in a different place.

Because ghosts emit negative emotional energy, it does not mean they are or were bad people. Their energy has nothing to do with their personalities. There are ghosts with good, helpful, or calm personalities who have chosen to remain behind but they still absorb and emit negative emotional energy. That's just the nature of being a ghost. Again, that's another reason to cross ghosts over and clear your home of a paranormal presence.

Spirits and Emotional Energy

In the afterlife, it's all about location, location, location. Ghosts are earthbound and usually stay fixed to a physical location. Spirits have crossed into the light and can come back to Earth any time to visit their living loved ones. Most people and animals that pass cross over and become spirits.

Once a ghost has crossed over and they become a spirit it that opens new doors to them. No longer are they fixed in one place, and they have a lot more abilities to communicate with the living anywhere on Earth at any time.

When entities "cross into the light" they're basically joining the energies that run through the cosmos. Those energies can travel at amazing speeds. Think about the speed of light at 186,000 miles per second! Spirits gain the ability to move that fast or faster and can appear in multiple places at the same time around the Earth. My theory about that is because energy is all connected. When a spirit appears in one place there's an energy tether that enables another part of their energy to appear in another location at the same time.

Spirit are entities of positive emotional energy. Spirits, like those of our loved ones feed off positive emotions like love, hope, and faith. That's why if you're missing someone who passed and aching for them in your heart, you're giving the spirit an emotional battery of positive energy to draw from and make an appearance in some way. While they absorb positive emotional energy, they also emit it. That's why when the spirit of a loved one is around you, you feel comfort and peace. You feel protected and as if you're being guided to do something- and you are.

Ghosts and Spirits Can Appear in Different Ways
The simplest form a ghost or spirit can take is in the shape of an orb. An orb is a rounded ball of light, like ectoplasm. Orbs usually have colors and designs in them, and that's the best way that I distinguish them from insects, reflections, pollen or dust in video and photographs.

Sometimes you can see a face in an orb. On one of my investigations a photo of an orb revealed the face of one of two women murdered in a home. That photo appears in my book "Lessons Learned from Talking to the Dead."

In addition to orbs, ghosts and spirits can also appear as dark shadows or shadow people.

Dark Entities
Dark entities or shadow people are basically just ghosts or spirits who do not have enough energy to manifest in full-color. As a result, they appear as a shadow. Think of having just enough dim light to be able to see the outline of a living person in your home. When you turn the lights brighter, you're able to see colors and features on the person. It's the same thing with a ghost. The more energy they are able to siphon, the clearer and more colorful they will appear.

Demons or Non-ghosts
Demons are not ghosts. They are energies from life forms that were never human or animal. Usually, they emit a great fear whenever they are around. Some people call them "demons." I believe that they are

energies from life forms that live in other solar systems.

As a scientist I know that science has found over 4,400 exoplanets or planets outside our solar system. Some appear to have the ingredients to create life (such as the Trappist-1 solar system that has a couple of planets in the habitable zone. Google it!). Scientists look at the atmosphere of these planets using light broken into different wavelengths (and colors) of the spectrum. The practice is called spectroscopy where different gases appear at different wavelengths in the spectrum. We would be foolish to think that there is no other planet in the cosmos that supports life, and I believe that what we call "dark entities are simply the "ghosts" or "spirits" of lifeforms from other universes.

So why would a "demon" or extra-terrestrial life form be hostile to humans? That's easy. If they're from another place (solar system) they won't understand what we are and could likely see us as a threat, and may take a defensive or sometimes offensive tact with people. It would be the same as how we may see a wild animal as a threat to our safety. They don't know what we're capable of, so they may be defensive.

Now that we've discussed various aspects of ghosts and spirits, I will explain the difference between an intelligent and residual haunt. We'll do that in the next chapter.

Chapter 3:
Hauntings: Residual Versus Intelligent

During my visits to England I ran into both residual and intelligent haunts. It's important to know the difference between the hauntings because you'll get answers from one and not from the other. In short, the difference between residual and intelligent hauntings is interaction.

Intelligent Hauntings
If you are in a place where you sense an earth-bound ghost and it reacts when you ask the entity to do something, then you have an intelligent and interactive ghost. Any ghost that can respond to a question is a sign of an intelligent haunting.

Paranormal television programs usually address only intelligent hauntings. They don't talk about residual hauntings because they usually don't have mediums that can sense energy left behind that doesn't interact.

Paranormal teams ask ghosts questions and use scientific equipment to obtain a direct response either through manipulation of electrical devices, a voice on a digital recorder that answers a question, or the detection of a thermal anomaly or magnetic field in a strange area. An intelligent haunt is basically like talking to a physical person who can respond. The person, however, happens to be dead and an earth-bound ghost.

Residual Hauntings

To best understand residual hauntings, think of the emotions that soldiers experience on a battlefield. During periods of extreme anxiety, fear, anger or joy people emit a lot of energy through their emotions. That energy, if great enough can mark a spot and linger through time. It's like a thumbprint on a window. It's something left behind, and only appears when sunlight (energy) shines through it. That thumbprint or residual energy can be increased by a living person's emotional energy, or physical energy like heat or light.

When people visit battlefields like Gettysburg in Pennsylvania, they have reported seeing Union and Confederate soldiers, hearing the sounds of battle or a bugle. That's because the emotional energy from the visitors is "charging" up that thumbprint of residual energy enough to materialize. People have also reported seeing mist or ectoplasm over the battlefields, which is basically a lot of residual energy.

Residual "haunts" don't have to be bad events, just events that generated a high level of emotions. As discussed earlier, emotional energy can be created from good and bad emotions. Emotions like fear, anger, anxiety and depression are negative emotions and generate negative energy. Love, faith and hope are positive emotions that generate positive emotional energy. The latter are used by spirits, not earth-bound ghosts.

One example of a residual haunt would be to see an image of a woman in a gown walking down a staircase who disappears at the bottom of the stair. In many homes, such figures have been reported. In this example, it's residual energy imprinted on the stairway area from a happy memory. Perhaps the woman of the house was dressed for an evening event and it was the night of her life. She would have left an "energy imprint" on that staircase throughout time. That imprint can come out again when a living person goes near that area of emotional energy, because their own emotional energy adds to it. That additional energy would enable the residual image to appear over and over again.

(Photo: Rob outside Windsor Castle.
Credit: R. Gutro)

When paranormal investigators encounter what they believe to be a residual haunt, they treat it as an intelligent haunt and ask questions. If they get no responses on their scientific equipment and if the image repeats itself in the same manner, they know they likely have a residual haunt.

Keep this difference in mind as you read about my encounters with the ghosts of England. I ran into both intelligent and residual haunts throughout my vacations.

How do Ghosts or Spirits Attach Energy to an Object?

Objects at rest have stored or residual energy. Think about Albert Einstein's Theory of Relativity, also known as the equation $E=mc2$. The equation means energy equals mass times distance squared. The energy that is intrinsically stored in a piece of matter at rest equals its mass times the speed of light squared.

There is actually a huge amount of energy stored in even little pieces of matter. Remember that the speed of light (186,000 miles per second) squared is an incredibly large number.

Earth-bound ghosts and spirits who have crossed over likely leave some of their emotional energy behind on objects that they had some attachment to in life. The attachment may not necessarily be for a good reason. As mentioned earlier, it's like an energy/emotional thumbprint. It just takes energy to make it re-appear.

Residual Energy in Furniture

In Ellicott City, Maryland an old rocking chair sitting outside of an antique store has been known to rock on its own. That's because there's an emotional attachment of the person to whom it belonged. If the person is an earthbound ghost (an intelligent haunt), they're likely sitting in the chair and waiting for a source of energy, either emotional or physical to provide them with the ability to rock the chair.

If the emotional imprint is from a spirit who has crossed into the light, energy near the object can draw them back to it. Think of it as leaving a little piece of you behind on an object, and when there's energy near it, the energy acts as a magnet to the spirit to come back to it. Spirits may want to return to an object just to let living people how much it meant to them.

Energy in Objects
Energy can also become attached to an object just like static electricity can build up in a woolen sweater. Think of objects that you love. Your love for an object attaches energy to the object like putting a thumbprint on glass. If people love something, like the house they live in- they will stay there in the afterlife. I've found that to be the case with a number of historic homes that I've visited.

Spirits and Objects
For spirits who have crossed over and had loved an object, they may have left some residual energy on it. If that object is with a living person who also has a love for it and the person in spirit, their love (emotional energy) will act as a beacon to call the spirit of the loved one to them.

Having someone's belonging such as their jewelry or their ashes will act as a magnet to bring a spirit back from time to time. I have the ashes of my two dogs who passed (Buzz and Sprite) and they both come back from time to time to let us know they're still around.

Ghosts and Objects

Earth-bound ghosts can actually attach themselves to an object as well as a location, but it's not too common. That means wherever the object goes, the ghost accompanies it. The ghost can be "awakened" if there is an energy source to empower them.

If you have an object in your home that has a ghost attached to it, your emotional energy and the physical energies (heat, light, water, electricity) in your home are acting as a battery to energize that ghost. In one instance, a woman who died on a mattress attached herself to the mattress and I had to cross her over.

Remove any object from your home that may have a ghostly attachment and return it to where it came from or bury it. You should also seek assistance to cross the ghost over into the light.

Now that you have a good base understanding of ghosts, spirits, their similarities and differences, you'll meet the ghosts of England in the next part of this book.

person is an earthbound ghost (an intelligent haunt), they're likely sitting in the chair and waiting for a source of energy, either emotional or physical to provide them with the ability to rock the chair.

If the emotional imprint is from a spirit who has crossed into the light, energy near the object can draw them back to it. Think of it as leaving a little piece of you behind on an object, and when there's energy near it, the energy acts as a magnet to the spirit to come back to it. Spirits may want to return to an object just to let living people how much it meant to them.

Energy in Objects

Energy can also become attached to an object just like static electricity can build up in a woolen sweater. Think of objects that you love. Your love for an object attaches energy to the object like putting a thumbprint on glass. If people love something, like the house they live in- they will stay there in the afterlife. I've found that to be the case with a number of historic homes that I've visited.

Spirits and Objects

For spirits who have crossed over and had loved an object, they may have left some residual energy on it. If that object is with a living person who also has a love for it and the person in spirit, their love (emotional energy) will act as a beacon to call the spirit of the loved one to them.

Having someone's belonging such as their jewelry or their ashes will act as a magnet to bring a spirit back from time to time. I have the ashes of my two dogs who passed (Buzz and Sprite) and they both come back from time to time to let us know they're still around.

Ghosts and Objects

Earth-bound ghosts can actually attach themselves to an object as well as a location, but it's not too common. That means wherever the object goes, the ghost accompanies it. The ghost can be "awakened" if there is an energy source to empower them.

If you have an object in your home that has a ghost attached to it, your emotional energy and the physical energies (heat, light, water, electricity) in your home are acting as a battery to energize that ghost. In one instance, a woman who died on a mattress attached herself to the mattress and I had to cross her over.

Remove any object from your home that may have a ghostly attachment and return it to where it came from or bury it. You should also seek assistance to cross the ghost over into the light.

Now that you have a good base understanding of ghosts, spirits, their similarities and differences, you'll meet the ghosts of England in the next part of this book.

PART 2:
ENCOUNTERS WITH THE
GHOSTS OF LONDON

Chapter 4:
The Ghost in the Jewel Tower

Britain's long history of bloody battles, grisly executions, and other intense emotionally saturated events help to keep the ghostly activity at a high level. Each day I encountered some kind of paranormal activity. Ghosts shared with me their names, their lives, why they were still here, and sometimes even their pain of death. I found the spiritual energy in London to be extremely active, so if you are sensitive to ghosts, you will find many restless entities still walking its streets.

The Jewel Tower was constructed in 1365 on land confiscated from Westminster Abbey for the specific purpose of safeguarding the private treasure of King Edward III. In 1512, during Henry VIII's reign, a fire destroyed the royal apartments and the royal jewels were relocated to another location.

Although the Tower ceased to be used as a royal residence, it continued to be used as a royal wardrobe until the 1600s. Parliament moved into the abandoned structures, and the Tower was used to store official records and other archival materials. The majority of the palace was destroyed again by yet another devastating fire in 1834. The Jewel Tower and Westminster Hall are all that remain of the original medieval palace.

*(Photo: Jewel Tower and Courtyard.
Credit: R. Gutro)*

Although the Tower was not open the day of my visit, it didn't have to be for me to see the ghost who haunts it.

As I walked past the Tower on my way to Westminster Abbey, I caught my first glimpse of the ghost. She was an elegantly dressed woman walking across the wrought iron fence-enclosed courtyard. I watched as the apparition crossed the grassy lawn and walk right through one of the Tower's thick stone walls, apparently through what had been a doorway at the time when the woman was alive.

The ghost had long brown hair, and wore a long crème-colored gown with a white collar. Unfortunately, I was unable to learn her name or why she was haunting the Tower's grounds, but I quickly drew a sketch of her.

(Sketch of the Jewel Tower Ghost. Credit: R. Gutro)

When I returned home from my trip, I investigated the clothing type worn by the apparition in an effort to determine the approximate time period when the woman might have lived. I was able to find a dress of similar style on the Bath and Somerset Council/Museum of Costume's website, and narrow down the time period to the 1660s. Whomever this woman was, she most likely served in the Palace of Westminster during this time period, and continues to walk the grounds where it once stood, even though very little of the original structure remains.

When visiting London's Jewel Tower, be sure to keep an eye out for the fashionably dressed female ghost who haunts its courtyard, and perhaps you may even be able to determine who she is and why she has decided to remain.

Chapter 5:
Many Ghosts of Westminster Abbey

Westminster Abbey has been a royal coronation church since 1066 A.D. It is the final resting place for seventeen monarchs and over 3,000 individuals not of noble birth. Daily religious rituals have been conducted on the site since Benedictine monks first settled here and constructed the first abbey in the middle of the tenth century. The current Gothic structure dates back to 1245.

(Photo: Westminster Abbey, St. John the Baptist Chapel, Exterior. Credit: R. Gutro)

The Ghost in the Churchyard
John Bradshaw was a lawyer, politician, and regicide. He was appointed lord president of the court that

presided over the trial and execution of King Charles I, which occurred on January 30, 1649, outside the Banqueting Hall of Whitehall Palace. Bradshaw died in 1659, and his remains were originally interred in the Abbey. When Charles II was restored to the throne, the bodies of all regicides buried within the abbey were disinterred and given gratuitous executions. Bradshaw's body was exhumed, drawn, and hung; his head put on a pike outside Westminster Hall. The bodies of the disinterred were later buried in a mass grave in churchyard of the neighboring church, St. Margaret's. Each year on the anniversary of the beheading of King Charles I, the ghost of John Bradshaw is said to appear and wander the grounds of the Abbey.

Henry VII Chapel
Construction of the Chapel started in 1503 with funding provided by the will of Henry VII. Henry's motivation was twofold: to venerate the Virgin Mary with the hope of being canonized himself, and legitimize his claim to the throne by providing a burial site for himself and his heirs. The structure was intended to be a sepulcher for only those with royal blood. However non-aristocrats were temporarily buried there, such as Oliver Cromwell and the bodies of those individuals were later disinterred during the Restoration. A partial list of the monarchs interred in the chapel includes Henry VII, Edward VI, Mary I, Elizabeth I, James I, William III and Mary II, Charles II, and Mary, Queen of Scots. Today, events such as installations of Knights of the Order of the Bath, and services to commemorate British Armed Servicemen are held here.

In the Henry VII Chapel, I sensed residual energy that consisted of tremendous fear and anxiety. I sensed that it was in this chapel where people during the Middle Ages who had recently learned they were going to be executed, would have offered up prayers to the Virgin Mary to be spared.

Tomb of Queen Elizabeth I

In the north aisle of the Henry VII Chapel lies the sarcophagus of Queen Elizabeth I. Elizabeth, daughter of King Henry VIII, was born at Greenwich Palace on September 7, 1533. She ascended the throne in 1558 upon the death of her half-sister, Mary I. Elizabeth's reign lasted 44 years; she would have been one of the longest reigning monarchs that people living at that time would have known. Because of this, Elizabeth would have been popularly loved by many of her subjects, so it is logical that there would be the emotional imprint of sorrow in this place. What's interesting to note is that this residual energy has lasted over 400 years, and, as with the Henry VII Chapel, is intensely palpable.

Ghost at the Tomb of Anne of Cleves

Anne of Cleves was the fourth wife of King Henry VIII. Their marriage lasted just six months, was never consummated, and she was never crowned queen consort. In exchange for a quick amicable divorce, Anne was granted the title of "King's Beloved Sister," and given houses and estates, including Hever Castle, the ancestral home of the Boleyns. It was at her tomb located in the choir of the abbey where I had a physical encounter.

(Photo: Westminster Abbey, Tomb of Anne of Cleves. Credit: R. Gutro)

I sensed a female entity standing between my husband Tom, and I. We were standing roughly ten feet apart. Tom was standing to the left side of the tomb and I was standing to the right. At the same instant, I felt a tugging of the hair on the left side of my head, and Tom felt the tugging of the hair on the right side of his head. It was as if the ghost was standing between us, with outstretched arms in either direction.

While I cannot confirm that it was indeed Anne of Cleves having a bit of fun with us that day, what I do know is that there was a ghost in the vicinity of her tomb who wanted to be noticed...and certainly got their wish.

Energy at the Marker of King Richard I

Richard was born on September 8, 1157, and was the third son of King Henry II. He was crowned at

Westminster Abbey in 1189 and died less than ten years later on April 6, 1199.

Richard was well educated, wrote poetry, and was fluent in both English and French. His military prowess during the Crusades is well documented; he is also the king associated with the Robin Hood stories.

During the siege of Châlus-Chabrol, Richard was inspecting the perimeter of the castle without armor, when he was wounded by a crossbowman defending the castle. The wound became gangrenous and he subsequently died. As a last act of chivalry, Richard pardoned the crossbowman responsible for his death, but the man was later executed when Richard died.

Richard's body was not buried in Westminster Abbey, but there is a marker commemorating his coronation. It was near this marker that I sensed a lot of residual energy: feelings of sadness, and intense grief. Richard's heart was removed from his corpse and is buried in Rouen Cathedral; his entrails are buried in Châlus-Chabrol. The rest of his remains were interred next to his father at Fontevraud Abbey in Anjou, France.

Poet's Corner Ghost
Poet's Corner is located in the South Transept of the Abbey. There you will find the final resting places of Henry James, Lewis Carroll, Dylan Thomas, Thomas Elliott, Alfred Lord Tennyson, George Elliott, D.H. Lawrence, Rudyard Kipling, Charles Dickens, and Geoffrey Chaucer.

However, the long impressive list of dead poets wasn't the only thing that caught my attention; I was distracted by the energy of a male ghost. This was not residual energy, but very much an intelligent haunt and very active.

The ghost told me that he died from a blow to the head in 1678, when he was 38 years old. He said he fell to the floor in that very area of the Abbey. He was confused when he awoke as energy, and tried to get help. But no one could hear him. He remains in Poet's Corner to this day.

Ghostly Monk in the Cloisters
In the Cloisters resides the ghostly apparition of a Benedictine monk named Father Benedictus. According to the website www.Ghost-Story.co.uk, Father Benedictus can be seen hovering above the floor. Over the years, the floor level has been progressively lowered, so the monk's ghost is seen "walking" at the elevation where the floor level once was, which is why he appears to be hovering in the air. So if you wish to catch a glimpse of the ghostly monk, it's best to arrive between five and six in the evening, the time of evening vespers.

Pyx Chamber Ghostly Monk's March
A pyx is a small box used to contain the consecrated host used in the communion ritual, and now lends its name to this room in the Abbey. The Pyx Chamber was once the sacristy of the original Edward the Confessor church that stood on this site. The oldest altar in the abbey has been moved to this room. Later

the room was used as a royal treasury, and the gold and silver used to mint coin was safeguarded here.

Sometimes when I touch objects, I get a visual image of the person or people that once handled that particular object. In this case, I touched a door in the Pyx Chamber that is probably hundreds of years old. Through my mind's eye, I "saw" robed monks walking around in the room. As they circled the room and passed by me, one by one, the monks would run their hands down the length of their robes. Not understanding the visage I was receiving, I looked around the room for a clue, and saw a wooden cope chest. I walked across the room to examine the chest more closely, and affixed to the lid of the chest was a plaque that read "Circa 1450. This cope chest stored monks' robes."

A Ghostly Poke in the Gift Shop

One of the last areas I visited in the Abbey was the gift shop. The shop was also part museum that had glass display cases with the effigies of queens and kings. Effigies are human-sized likenesses of the deceased used in the funeral processions. The figures are carved from wood and wax. Some of the facial features are incredibly life-like, having been created from death masks.

While looking at the displays, I was poked in my back. I turned around and no one was behind me, except for the ghost who did the poking. I did not get the ghost's name or find out why he was trying to get my attention. The only thing I was able to discern was that it was a male energy.

There are a lot of ghosts in Westminster Abbey. Some have remained because they love the Abbey and never want to leave; others linger behind by their own choice, perhaps atoning for what they consider to be wrongs committed when they were alive. In either case, you should never incite anger in a ghost. Treat them with respect. And if they attempt to make contact with you, more than likely they're trying to get your assistance to help cross them over.

Chapter 6:
Lord Moon of the Mall's Ghostly Patrons

To the British, enjoying a pint while sitting next to someone who used to frequent a pub when they were alive may not surprise them at all, but to visitors, it can be a tad bit unnerving.

The *Lord Moon of the Mall* is located on Whitehall Street in London. It's a good place to take a break from sightseeing and tip back a pint or two. Apparently, there were men and women in the afterlife who were also enjoying a drink.

(Photo: Lord Moon of the Mall, Menu. Credit: R. Gutro)

When visiting a British pub, there are a few American norms that one must forgo. Immediately upon entering, it is important to first choose a table, and memorize the number affixed to the table. After reviewing the menu, food orders are placed at the bar, and assigned to the table number. Once prepared, the food will be brought out to your table. Drinks are immediately served from the bar, which you then carry back to the table. Don't make the mistake of waiting to be seated, or better yet, waiting at a table for a waiter or waitress to serve you because you'll be waiting a long time!

Immediately upon entering the pub, my characteristic headache returned, indicating to me that there was a ghost among the patrons.

So I started taking photographs in succession, while pointing the camera in the direction of where I sensed the energy. In one of the photos, several orbs are clearly visible. A review of the photos showed that orbs were present in only one photograph, and not in the photos snapped immediately before and immediately after the one with the orbs. That's my own personal way of making the determination that the objects are truly "orbs," and not dust, pollen, or reflections.

*(Photo: Lord Moon of the Mall, Interior.
Credit: R. Gutro)*

As discussed previously, orbs are the simplest manifestation that a ghost (or spirit) can take.

While on paranormal investigations, photos taken of orbs are a good way to confirm the presence of an energy, and also confirm what I'm sensing. In this particular case, the number of orbs in the photograph indicated that there was more than one ghost attempting to order drinks that day in the pub. Without a doubt, some were attempting to make their presence known to the staff. I would have liked the opportunity to interview some of the pub staff.

One of the ghosts actually identified himself by name. As a medium, I "hear" things telepathically. I distinctly heard a male voice tell me that his name was Andrew. He said that he lived in the early 1700s and operated a business out of the same structure where the pub is today. From the images that Andrew was relaying, my interpretation was that Andrew's business was a butcher's shop.

Andrew did not reveal why he was there, but I sensed that he worked hard to make his business a success, and that he continues working to this day.

When I returned from vacation, I made an attempt to learn more about the establishments that operated out of Whitehall Street, but was unable to confirm the existence of Andrew's business.

(Photo: Lord Moon of the Mall, Interior. Image with multiple orbs. Credit: R. Gutro)

A few days later, I returned to the pub to see if I could learn more about the ghosts. Andrew's ghost did not come forward a second time. Ghosts, just like people, talk to whom they want, when they want, and Andrew apparently was not in the mood to be sociable.

(Photo: Lord Moon of the Mall, Interior. Credit: R. Gutro)

As discussed previously, orbs are the simplest manifestation that a ghost (or spirit) can take.

While on paranormal investigations, photos taken of orbs are a good way to confirm the presence of an energy, and also confirm what I'm sensing. In this particular case, the number of orbs in the photograph indicated that there was more than one ghost attempting to order drinks that day in the pub. Without a doubt, some were attempting to make their presence known to the staff. I would have liked the opportunity to interview some of the pub staff.

One of the ghosts actually identified himself by name. As a medium, I "hear" things telepathically. I distinctly heard a male voice tell me that his name was Andrew. He said that he lived in the early 1700s and operated a business out of the same structure where the pub is today. From the images that Andrew was relaying, my interpretation was that Andrew's business was a butcher's shop.

Andrew did not reveal why he was there, but I sensed that he worked hard to make his business a success, and that he continues working to this day.

When I returned from vacation, I made an attempt to learn more about the establishments that operated out of Whitehall Street, but was unable to confirm the existence of Andrew's business.

(Photo: Lord Moon of the Mall, Interior. Image with multiple orbs. Credit: R. Gutro)

A few days later, I returned to the pub to see if I could learn more about the ghosts. Andrew's ghost did not come forward a second time. Ghosts, just like people, talk to whom they want, when they want, and Andrew apparently was not in the mood to be sociable.

So when in London, be sure to visit the Lord Moon of the Mall pub. Be sensitive to the ghosts that linger there, and be sure to take lots of pictures because the ghostly haunts abound. I also sense that after the pub closes, the socializing continues.

Chapter 7:
A Ghostly Congregation at St. Paul's Cathedral

St. Paul's Cathedral with its iconic dome is one of the most famous and easily recognized landmarks in London's skyline. The English-Baroque structure is actually the fifth to occupy the central city site since the year 604 AD.

Designed by Sir Christopher Wren in 1675, the Cathedral was constructed in just 35 years to replace its predecessor that was destroyed in the Great Fire in 1666.

*(Photo: St. Paul's Cathedral, Exterior.
Credit: R. Gutro)*

For a small fee, visitors can climb to the cupola on top of the Cathedral's dome and take in spectacular panoramic views of London. Because of my fear of heights, I confess that I did not make the ascent to the cupola. However, the views from the observation deck at the dome's base are almost as splendid.

(Photo: St. Paul's Cathedral, View from the Stone Gallery. Credit: R. Gutro)

Without a doubt, given the age of the Cathedral, and the number of structures that have stood on the very same site, the place is haunted. When ghosts choose a location, for the most part, they're bound to it. Ghosts who inhabited any one of the previous structures, in all likelihood, still remain and occupy the current one.

As with pretty much all religious houses of worship, the Cathedral is filled with a lot of residual emotional energy. All that is needed for a residual or intelligent haunt to manifest itself is for the physical or emotional energies of a living person to be present and provide the necessary energy from which to draw.

Churches have ghosts for a myriad of possible reasons, but I'd like to propose the following. First, a person may have been very religious in life and was totally dedicated to their church. As a result of their dedication, even after their physical death, they chose not to leave. Second, when we die, we have an awakening and recall all of our life experiences. If, during this awakening a devoutly religious person misinterprets something that they may have done while they were living as being terrible or evil, they may fear crossing over in the afterlife so they choose to stay earthbound as a ghost and risk the potential of spending an eternity in an unfortunate place. Of course, there's nothing but love, peace, forgiveness and healing on the other side, so their fear is unjustified.

Father Jonathan's Ghost
Immediately upon entering the Cathedral's west end, my characteristic headache returned. I sensed the presence of a ghost, someone who had been a holy man in life, as in a priest or monk. It was then that I "heard" the name Father Jonathan. Immediately after receiving the name, I got a clear picture of what Father Jonathan looked like as the ghost projected his visage to me: he was an elderly man, bald, and with a beard.

In addition to the priest, there were many other ghosts present. Because of the large number of entities, it was very difficult to get more information from Father Jonathan. Imagine a large number of people, all shouting at you at the same time, vying for your undivided attention. In spite of what little information I was able to get from Father Jonathan, I was later able to get a confirmation of his ghost.

When I returned to the States, I conducted research to learn more about the existence of a Father Jonathan. The www.themortonreport.com reports that St. Paul's is haunted by the ghost of an elderly clergyman; his presence is accompanied by "tuneless whistling." I unfortunately didn't hear the whistling during my visit because of all the ambient noise. The ghost is known to haunt the All Souls' Chapel located in the northwest tower, which is exactly the area of the Cathedral where I encountered him.

Later, on the same vacation, I had the opportunity to attend a walking tour of central London with Richard Jones, noted author of several paranormal books in the U.K. Richard was able to confirm that the description of the ghost I had seen was identical to the description of an apparition that appeared to a Cathedral docent.

The Cathedral was very impressive, and a definite must-see destination when you're in London. When you visit, if you are fortunate to hear the whistling Father Jonathan, be sure to wish him well.

Chapter 8:
Ghost Dog in
Sir John Soane's Museum

Arguably one of the most famous British architects ever was Sir John Soane (1753–1837). His home in London is now a museum, and houses a wealth of architectural fragments, artifacts from the antiquities, and priceless works of art.

Whenever Soane would acquire a new piece, it was not uncommon for him to throw lavish parties where as many as 800 guests would cram into the tight accommodations of his row house just to catch a glimpse of the item. If he was only able to acquire one of an item, and he desired two, Soane would commission a replica of the first to complete the pairing. As an architect, Soane was known for his original and unique application of the neo-classical style; many of his commissions are now protected as historic landmarks and include the Bank of England (London), the Royal Hospital (Chelsea), St. Peter's Church (Walworth), and a long list of country houses.

Upon entering the front door of the museum, I immediately sensed a ghost, but this time it wasn't the ghost of a human. It was the ghost of a dog. As I reviewed the exhibits, I learned the dog's identity, found her grave, and even found her image in a painting.

(Photo: Sir John Soane Museum, Exterior. Credit: R. Gutro)

In the center of the museum is a small interior courtyard called "the Monk's Yard." The courtyard is open to the sky, and contains a Soane-design monument with the words "Alas, Poor Fanny" engraved on its face. As I entered the museum's portrait gallery, I received confirmation that "Fanny" was indeed the dog's name.

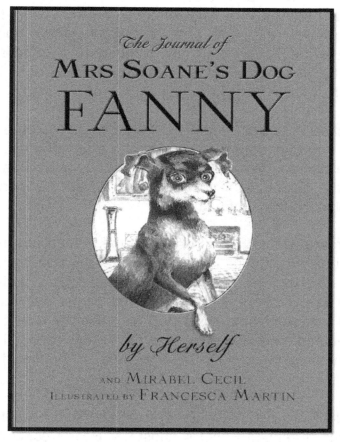

(Book: The Journal of Mrs. Soane's Dog Fanny by Mirabel Cecil and Francesca Martin)

In the gallery hangs a large portrait of Mrs. Soane with Fanny resting comfortably on her lap. I took a picture of the painting so that I could recall Fanny's likeness.

While perusing the museum's gift shop, I happened upon a book entitled *"The Journal of Mrs. Soane's Dog Fanny."* Of course, I had to purchase it. The book chronicles the adventures of Fanny and her friend Mew (the name of the cat that lived next door). Written by Mirabel Cecil and illustrated by Francesca Martin, it is intended to be a children's book, but adults will also enjoy reading it.

I asked the clerk, whom I will refer to as Margaret, if she had ever sensed the ghost of a dog in the house. She replied, "Yes." She said that several occupants of the house after the Soanes had also reported seeing the ghost of a dog.

Margaret went on to explain that the homeowner that occupied the house immediately after the Soanes had two Dachshunds that were always anxious, agitated, and would never settle down. The owner eventually had to send the dogs to live elsewhere. She attributed the behavior of the living dogs had something to do with the presence of the ghost of Fanny.

I told Margaret that while in the basement exhibition space, I sensed Fanny's ghost. Margaret confirmed that Fanny has indeed been seen numerous times running around in the basement.

Margaret asked if I had sensed the ghost of a person in the house; I told her I did not. She confirmed that this was consistent with what other museum employees and former owners believed; there has never been any experiences with a human ghost.

Although I didn't expect the ghost of a dog to come through to me, Fanny made sure that I knew she was there. I sensed that although Mr. and Mrs. Soane had crossed over, Fanny would be forever happy running around in her home.

Chapter 9:
Sickly Ghosts at the Banqueting House

Located a short walking distance from No. 10 Downing Street and Trafalgar Square, the Banqueting House is the only original component of the Palace of Whitehall that survives. At the end of Henry VIII's reign in 1547, Whitehall Palace was huge, covering an area of 23 acres, making it the largest royal palace in Europe at that time. All that changed, however, on January 12, 1619, when a devastating fire destroyed a significant portion of the palace. Later that same year, sparing no expense, the Banqueting House was rebuilt, designed by the famous British architect Inigo Jones in the new fashionable neo-classical style.

(Photo: The Banqueting House, Exterior. Credit: R. Gutro)

Today, the Banqueting House is used as both a museum and venue space.

(Photo: The Banqueting House, Interior.
Credit: R. Gutro)

The large two-story events space is located on the second level. The ceiling of this room features an original masterpiece painted by Sir Peter Paul Rubens. The painting is comprised of three sections entitled *"The Union of the Crowns," "The Apotheosis of James I,"* and *"The Peaceful Reign of James I."* On the lower level, located directly beneath the banqueting hall, is a vaulted space known as the undercroft. This area was used as a drinking den by King James I and his friends.

King Charles I believed in the Divine Right of Kings. Sometimes also called the royal prerogative, this belief holds that sovereigns are anointed by God, and that all authority to govern belongs solely to the monarchy. As you can imagine, this kind of resolute thinking was bound to cause friction.

(Photo: Tom inside the Banqueting House. Credit: R. Gutro)

After a bloody Civil War (1642-1649) and protracted power struggle between Parliament and the king, Charles I was put on trial; he was found guilty of treason and sentenced to death. A scaffold was constructed immediately outside the Banqueting House on the side fronting onto Whitehall Street. On January 30, 1649, Charles I was beheaded. Immediately after the execution, eyewitness accounts cite that observers dipped their handkerchiefs in the blood of the king, believing that it possessed healing properties. Every year on the anniversary of this event, the Banqueting House holds a memorial service to commemorate the only time that Britain has ever executed one of its sovereigns.

Although Charles I was executed directly outside the building, his ghost does not tarry inside. However, there are other ghosts that reside within.

As I entered the building, I immediately felt my throat go dry and get sore. The first thing a paranormal investigator does is assume that everything has a logical explanation. So I dismissed my symptoms as being attributable to atmospheric conditions inside the building.

King Charles II, son of Charles I, believed that he had "the royal touch." That is, the ability to cure the sick. Charles thought that he could heal people afflicted with a malady of the throat called Scapula simply by the laying on of hands. The symptoms of Scapula include a dry, sore, and swollen throat; these symptoms matched what I felt! Connecting all the points – the symptoms that I felt, the symptoms associated with Scapula, the royal touch – this indicated to me that some of the people who came to the Banqueting House to be healed by the king, later died, and were still wandering around as ghosts looking for a cure to their sickness.

While I could not confirm the number of ghosts who are wandering around inside the Banqueting House, it is certain that there is definitely more than one. These are intelligent haunts, or interactive ghosts.

Residual energy can make you feel uneasy, but it takes an intelligent haunt to convey the exact symptoms of an illness at the time of a person's passing. The ghosts are those of people who died hoping to get cured from Charles II, and decided to stay because they're still waiting for the cure.

Chapter 10:
Ghosts of Guild Hall

Guild Hall

Guild Hall was built in 1411, and has been in continuous use for civic purposes for hundreds of years. The structure miraculously survived the Great Fire of London in 1666, most likely due to its stone construction. It is still the ceremonial and administrative center for the City of London.

(Photo: Guild Hall, Exterior. Credit: www.pinterest.com)

During the Roman period, the site was the location of an amphitheater, the outline of which is marked by black-colored stones in the pavement of the forecourt.

Guild Hall was the location of many famous court proceedings, including the trials of Lady Jane Grey and her husband, Robert Guilford.

A tragic story, for certain, Lady Jane Grey was queen of England for just 9 days – from July 10 to July 19, 1553. She was a first cousin of Edward VI; her grandmother was Henry VIII's sister – Princess Mary. To ensure that the throne passed on to another Protestant, King Edward IV designated Lady Jane as his heir, totally by-passing his half-sister Mary. Since Jane was just 15 years old at the time, it is reasonable to assume that her actions were being manipulated by others. Mary Tudor marched on London with her army, and Lady Jane surrendered without any bloodshed. She and her husband were tried, convicted of treason, and executed on February 12, 1554.

Other notable trials that took place in Guild Hall are listed on a large wall plaque, and include Anne Askew, Protestant martyr; Francis Dereham and Thomas Culpeper, paramours of Catherine Howard (Henry VIII's fifth wife), and Henry Garnet (co-conspirator in the Guy Fawkes' Gunpowder Plot).

The paranormal energy inside the hall is residual. On my visit, I did not sense an intelligent haunt – a ghost who could interact with the living. There was, however, a tremendous amount of emotional energy, most likely left from the many historic events that have taken place within its walls. When residual energy has been impressed upon a location, it remains dormant until the presence of physical energy is present to activate it.

(Photo: Guild Hall, Interior. Credit: www.pinterest.com)

I have to admit that I find it ironic that I did not encounter an intelligent haunt inside Guild Hall. I did, however, encounter interactive ghosts lingering just outside of the building.

Ghost in the Doorway

After leaving Guild Hall, I encountered the ghostly figure of a man standing in the doorway of a neighboring building. He was leaning with his back up against the wall, wearing a dark cloak and tall hat. His knee was bent, leg raised, and his foot on the wall. When I looked again, he instantly vanished. I knew that I had just seen a ghost, but I was unable to find out any more information about him.

*(Image: Sketch of the Ghost in the Doorway.
Credit: R. Gutro)*

When I returned to Guild Hall the following day, I passed by the same doorway, and had a second encounter with the very same ghostly apparition. This time, I took pictures of the doorway, and captured an image with three orbs.

For certain, one of the orbs in the picture is the ghost of the man in the doorway that I saw the previous night.

(Photo: View of Orbs. Credit: R. Gutro)

After returning to the States, I scoured the Internet for an image that matched the sketch I had drawn. I was successful at confirming that the clothing type matched what was typical for the early 1600s.

This time period coincides with the Gunpowder Plot of 1605 – Guy Fawkes' ill-fated attempted to blow up the Parliament building with gunpowder stowed in the basement. Since Henry Garnets' trial took place in nearby Guild Hall, could this have been his apparition?

It would be fun to think that it might be, but a much longer investigation would be necessary to confirm exactly who this man was. What I find interesting is that I was able to return to the exact same location on two separate occasions, encounter the same apparition, and confirm the presence of his ghost with a photograph of an orb. Whoever this man was, apparently that's his corner. So be sure to look for the ghost in the doorway the next time you're in the vicinity of Guild Hall.

Chapter 11:
Hauntings of St. Bartholomew's Hospital and the Viaduct Pub

St. Bartholomew's Hospital
St. Bartholomew's Hospital, also referred to as "Barts," was founded in 1123, by a man named Rahere, a favorite courtier of King Henry I.

(Photo: St. Bartholomew's Hospital, Exterior. Credit: R. Gutro)

In addition to being an active teaching hospital, Barts also houses an extensive archive and museum collection documenting the advancements in patient care, the training of doctors and healthcare practitioners, and hospital administration since the 12th century.

Barts is also known as the place where Sir Arthur Conan Doyle's Sherlock Holmes character, in the novel *"A Study in Scarlet,"* met his sidekick Dr. John Watson for the first time.

St. Bartholomew's Hospital has provided healthcare for almost 900 years. That also means that a lot of patients have died in the hospital. Sometimes when people pass away in hospitals they linger as ghosts. That's because they "wake up" as energy and are confused. Sometimes, even though they may see the light they may wander around in confusion and not cross over, causing them to remain earthbound, at least until they can be helped to go into the light. Such is the case in Barts.

As paranormal investigators, it is important to respect the people and places where we conduct research. I did not actually go into Barts, however, the energy emanating from the structure was very palpable, even when standing outside and taking photographs.

The Viaduct Pub's Ghosts
The Viaduct Pub was built in 1869 on the site of the Giltspur Comptor – a debtors' prison.

Five of the original holding cells survive in the pub's basement, however, this area is off limits to patrons. One of the ghosts that haunts the pub is in the cellar. Another ghost haunts the first floor.

In 1996, a pub manager experienced the basement haunting. The story he tells is that the door to the upstairs suddenly slammed shut and all of the lights went out. Fortunately, his wife was on the first floor and heard him yelling for help. The manager found his way to the door in the dark, but it wouldn't open from his side. When his wife arrived, she was able to easily open the door from the outside. Apparently, the ghost in the basement wanted the pub manager to stay, possibly to communicate with him.

(Photo: The Viaduct Pub, Exterior.
Credit: R. Gutro)

When I visited the pub, it was full of patrons enjoying drinks and eating. Living people create a lot of emotional energy, which sometimes makes it hard for a medium to zero in on an earthbound ghost.

However, I could sense a lot of energy in the pub. I learned that pub employees have seen a male ghost and call him "Fred."

Richard Jones, author and Walking Haunted London tour guide, recounts the story of a televised event in the pub where a medium was told nothing about the history of the pub or any haunting. The medium said, "There is a Scotsman here named Robert. He asks that people stop calling him 'Fred!'"

Chapter 12:
Ghost Judge of St. Mary's Churchyard

St. Mary's Churchyard is located on St. Mary's Road in Wimbledon. Roman artifacts recovered from property indicate that it had once been the site of an Anglo-Saxon settlement. The graveyard contains the remains of soldiers from World Wars I and II.

The first record of a church building on the site is documented in the Domesday Book from 1086. By the end of the thirteenth century, a new church had been built on the site; the ruins visible today are the remains of that structure.

(Photo: St. Mary's Churchyard. Credit: R. Gutro)

Hanging Judge Hawkins' Ghost

When I entered the cemetery, I immediately sensed the presence of a male ghost, confirming reports that the ghost of Judge Henry Hawkins haunts the cemetery. Hawkins lived from 1817 to 1907. His remains are not interred here, but rather in Kensal Green Cemetery. One plausible explanation for why Judge Hawkins' ghost haunts the churchyard is that the court building where Hawkins presided was once located in the vicinity.

Sometimes a ghost will linger in an area they frequented in life. I believe that's why the ghost of Judge Hawkins haunts this cemetery. He's not really haunting the cemetery itself, but rather he's haunting the location where the courthouse once stood, the site of which has now been incorporated into the cemetery.

Here's how that works: if a ghost decides to take up residence in a house where he/she grew up, and the house is later torn down, the ghost would seek the next closest structure. I believe that's what happened with Judge Hawkins. His ghost has been seen walking around in the churchyard, often holding papers.

Once I felt his presence, I began taking multiple pictures. In one photograph, I captured the image of several orbs. It makes sense to me that one of the orbs would be Judge Hawkins; I am uncertain as to the identity of the other orbs.

(Photo: St. Mary's Churchyard, Image of Orbs.
Credit: R. Gutro)

For some reason, Judge Hawkins has decided to stay behind as an earthbound ghost. Perhaps he regrets the final dispositions of cases he tried, and seeks forgiveness for his ruling. Perhaps he loved being a judge and wanted to stay there in the afterlife. Whatever the reason may be, when visiting St. Mary's Churchyard, be on the lookout for the ghost of Judge Hawkins.

Chapter 13:
The Ghostly Greeters of
Pewterers' Hall

Pewterers' Hall is located on Oat Lane in London. The earliest documented reference to the hall was dated 1348. King Edward IV granted the first charter in 1473-1474, which gave the company the rights govern the trade of pewter throughout the kingdom, in perpetuity. There's quite a bit more to the company and Pewterers' Hall history, so I encourage you to visit their website. Today, the principal activities of the Pewterers' Company are to support England's pewter trade, manage its charities, and support the City of London government and the Armed Forces of the Crown.

On a small grass-covered area behind Pewterers' Hall, our tour guide stopped and started explaining to the group the history of the building. It was here that I sensed several ghosts and developed my characteristic headache. I told our tour guide that I felt as if we were standing in a cemetery. There were several ghosts who were telling me that their remains were located where we were standing.

The message seemed odd to me because the area in which we were standing didn't look like a cemetery there were no clues of an ancient structure like a church or any indications at all that the site served as a burial ground at any time. Since Pewterers' Hall no ruins, fences, stone walls that define a perimeter that has stood on this site for such a long period of time, I thought the chances of having a cemetery directly behind it were slim.

But when questioned, our tour guide confirmed there were indeed many unmarked graves under our feet, which subsequently confirmed the messages I was receiving from the ghosts.

(Photo: Pewterers' Hall, Exterior. Image of multiple orbs. Credit: R. Gutro)

I realized our presence and the emotional energy we brought with us enabled a number of ghosts to materialize.

Immediately, I began taking multiple pictures. Several of the photos showed nothing at all, but in one there were dozens of orbs. Unfortunately, since we were on a walking tour, I didn't have time to conduct an investigation.

As an aside, cemeteries generally are not haunted places. The only time entities appear is when a living person is nearby, bringing with them their own emotional energy. That energy can be used to help an earthbound ghost or spirit appear or communicate with the living. Apparently, there were a number of earthbound ghosts lingering around their physical remains in that location.

I've mentioned previously that ghosts often choose to frequent a place where they lived, worked, or died. In this case, the ghosts wanted to stay near their remains. It's likely that the ghosts went to where their remains were buried because the actual physical structure in which they had previously chosen to spend their eternity had been destroyed. Ghosts can be drawn to their physical remains because of residual energy in those remains. Similarly, spirits are also drawn to their ashes.

Communicating with those who have passed takes a lot of time and concentration, and takes much more time than what is typically allotted on a walking tour. That's why paranormal investigators spend hours in a haunted location. As a medium, messages come through (often telepathically) as individual words, pictures, or names, and it takes time to piece them together. It also requires a lot of concentration to focus on one particular entity. Since there were many ghosts behind Pewterers' Hall, I could not focus on one as they were all talking to me at once.

Hopefully, a paranormal team will investigate the area, determine the messages, and cross over those ghosts who want to transition. That's something that would require some time.

I was unable to confirm if there are ghosts who haunt the inside of Pewterers' Hall, but given the number of ghosts that were present outside, we had enough to keep us busy.

Chapter 14:
The Ghostly Monk of St. Bartholomew's

St. Bartholomew-the-Great is one of London's oldest churches. The church was founded in 1123 as an Augustinian Priory. When the monasteries were dissolved under Henry VIII, it remained a parish church, but sections of the structure were used for housing and storage. Today, it's an active Anglican Church.

(Photo: St. Bartholomew the Great Church, Exterior. Credit: R. Gutro)

The building is very attractive and has been used as a set in several films, including two that I've enjoyed:

"Elizabeth: the Golden Age" and "The Other Boleyn Girl."

Local legend says that a monk named Rahere haunts the church; he was the monk who founded the priory and his remains have been interred inside the church.

Rahere's crypt was opened in 1865 during building renovations. The skeleton of the monk was found to be intact as were the sandals on his feet. A laborer working on the renovations broke into the crypt and removed one of the sandals. Soon thereafter, the laborer became ill, and attempted to return the sandal. But when he returned to the crypt, he discovered that the skeleton had been moved, and the sandal could not be reunited with the rest of the skeleton. The story goes that it was around this time that the monk's ghost began haunting the church, perhaps searching for his missing sandal.

In May of 1999, a man named John Caster who lived near the church, was awakened by the church's alarm monitoring company and asked to investigate the cause for the alarm's activation; the church's laser beam system had been triggered. Caster found no one inside the locked building, and the only light beams that had been interrupted were those near Rahere's tomb. A living person would have to walk from one end of the church, and through other laser beams in order to reach the tomb, but no other beams had been interrupted. Could it have been Rahere's ghost that triggered the alarm?

The church was not open on my visit. But I didn't need to enter the church to find the monk's ghost because he came outside to greet us.

(Photo: St. Bartholomew the Great Church, Exterior. Image of orb. Credit: R. Gutro)

Only moments after I arrived, I sensed the presence of the male ghost. I looked over in the direction of the church and took several pictures. I pointed my camera in the direction of where I sensed the ghost to be standing. In one of photos, a large orb is visible, confirming the presence of the monk's ghost.

So if you find yourself in the area of St. Bartholomew's, be on the lookout for the ghostly monk searching for his missing sandal.

PART 3: ENCOUNTERS WITH MANY GHOSTS OF HAMPTON COURT PALACE

Chapter 15:
Ghosts Abound at Hampton Court Palace

Hampton Court Palace is located 40 miles southwest of London. Originally built by Cardinal Thomas Wolsey, the cardinal later gifted the palace to Henry VIII when he fell out of favor with the king. It is only one of two palaces owned by Henry VIII that survive to this day. Over a period of ten years, the king spent lavishly on improvements to the palace, making it one of the most modern and magnificent palaces in all of England.

(Photo: Hampton Court Palace, Exterior. Credit: R. Gutro)

After the death of Henry VIII, the palace fell out of royal favor and into disrepair. Two hundred years later, during the reign of William and Mary, large portions of the Tudor palace were pulled down and reconstructed in the more fashionable Baroque style of the day. Fortunately, a lack of finances and the deaths of William and Mary prevented any further destruction of the Tudor portions of the palace.

(Photo: Hampton Court Palace, Exterior.
Credit: R. Gutro)

The Great Hall and Great Watching Chamber
One of the most impressive and largest rooms in the palace is the Great Hall, designed by Queen Anne Boleyn, who personally supervised its construction. The room is 106 feet long and 40 feet wide; the ceiling is 60 feet high. Just about everything in this

room, from the stained glass window depicting the king and his six wives, the elegantly carved room divider, the hammer beam trusses holding up the roof, to the cloth of gold tapestries, is original and survives from the Tudor period.

This room did not have an intelligent haunt. However, the residual emotional energy impressed upon the space was palpable; energy that was generated by the emotions of the people who came here to dine with the king survive and linger. All of that energy is manifested when living people are present and provide their emotional energy.

I sensed an overwhelming positive energy, generated from musicians playing and lots of dancing. This is consistent with the use and purpose of the room. All of that positive energy quickly became dark and negative immediately upon leaving the Great Hall and entering the next room known as the Great Watching Chamber.

The Great Watching Chamber was also a large space. This room was designed by Queen Jane Seymour, and is filled with light pouring in through the original Tudor-period leaded glass windows. The walls are lined with seats where people would wait to see the king. And as with the Great Hall, large tapestries have been hung on each wall. I was fascinated by the tapestries not only because of their intricate detail, but because of their size; they spanned the full height of the space, from floor to ceiling.

The Great Watching Chamber did not have an interactive ghost either, but it did have a lot of residual energy. I sensed great anxiety and anticipation, which is consistent with energy that would be generated by people waiting for the king.

I exited this room and walked into a long hallway. It was in this space where I encountered one of the palace's most famous ghosts.

The Screaming Ghost in the Haunted Gallery

The most haunted space in Hampton Court Palace is purported to be the Haunted Gallery. The walls are lined with draperies from floor to ceiling, and large portraits have been hung on the walls, hence the name of the space. At one end of the gallery is the Great Watching Chamber; at the opposite end is the Council Chamber and Chapel Royal.

It was in a room off the gallery where Queen Catherine Howard was arrested. The story goes that she managed to break free from the guards and run down this very corridor, screaming the name of her husband, "Henry!"

As I entered the gallery, the audio tour description of the Great Watching Chamber was wrapping up, and I immediately developed my characteristic headache.

As I walked over to the drapery-lined wall, I sensed the ghost of a young woman running down the hallway and pass right through me. I was overcome with a feeling of abject terror.

(Photo: Hampton Court Palace, the Haunted Gallery. Credit: R. Gutro)

The audio tour description of the gallery began with the stories of visitors' reports of being touched by a ghostly hand reaching out from behind the tapestries; the very same ones where I had been standing when I had my encounter.

Others have reported seeing the figure of a woman, dressed in a white gown with long flowing hair, drifting down the gallery.

Hampton Court Palace's publication *"Is the Palace Haunted? Palace Phantoms,"* states that one person said of their experience with the ghost: "Just as she (the ghost) reaches the Royal Pew, she lets out an unearthly shriek and hurries back to the top of the stairs with a ghastly look of despair." When Catherine was queen, her apartments were once located at the top of the stairs mentioned in the quote.

Who Was Catherine Howard?

Perhaps a little history about Henry VIII's fifth queen, Catherine Howard, is in order since she continues to haunt the palace.

Catherine was born in 1523, and was the first cousin of Anne Boleyn, Henry VIII's second queen. At the age of five, Catherine's mother died and she was sent to live with her step-grandmother. Although Catherine received an education befitting her status, there was very little supervision, and she received an "education" in a few other areas as well. Catherine was brought to court by her power lusting family, where she caught the attention of the king. Henry was immediately smitten with the young Catherine, who he referred to as his "rose without a thorn." They were wed on July 28, 1540, almost immediately after the annulment of the king's marriage to Anne of Cleves. But Catherine wasn't queen for very long.

Less than two years later, some very shady characters at court learned about Catherine's colorful past. A past that revealed she was not a virgin, and that she had been having relations with two other young men at court; not an unrealistic scenario given that Catherine was in her late teens at the time, and Henry was in his late 40s.

She was charged with adultery, which happens to be treason if you're the queen. Catherine was tried, convicted, and executed along with her paramours. A very brutal ending for such a young girl.

(Photo: Hampton Court Palace, the Haunted Gallery. Credit: R. Gutro)

The Palace's Other Ghosts
The palace has 18 interior courtyards; three of which are purported to be haunted – Base Court, Clock Court, and Fountain Court. Nine different ghosts occupy these areas of the palace, and I ran into several of them during my visit.

Base Court's Lady in Grey
Base Court is the first interior courtyard entered after crossing the drawbridge across the moat, walking under the portcullis, and through the Great Gate House. Once I stepped into Base Court, I developed my characteristic headache. I was immediately drawn to one particular corner of the court. I sensed the presence of an entity, but couldn't figure out who it was. I later learned from other sources that the ghost of a Lady in Grey occupies that very corner of the court.

There have been several plausible suggestions as to the identity of the ghost. One suggestion is that the ghost is Mrs. Sybil Penn, nurse to King Edward VI (Henry VIII's son). Mrs. Penn died of smallpox at Hampton Court in 1568, and was buried in St. Mary's Church. Her grave was robbed and her bones scattered. It's possible that the ghost of Mrs. Penn has returned to haunt the place where she enjoyed living the most, but I believe that she's seeking assistance from the living in finding her lost bones.

Clock Court's Phantom Dog
Over the years, visitors to the palace have reported seeing a phantom dog. The dog is most often sighted

in the area of Clock Court, and barking has been heard in the King's Staircase located in the William and Mary section of the palace.

The phantom dog is said to resemble a mutt, and since most dogs were forbidden in the palace by Queen Victoria, the dog very likely was a resident of the palace prior to her reign.

(Photo: Hampton Court Palace, the King's Staircase. Credit: R. Gutro)

Clock Court's Hooded Figure
In October 2003, after the palace was closed for the day, closed-circuit television security cameras captured footage of what appears to be a hooded figure forcibly opening open a pair of doors located in the William III state apartments. By the time security personnel reached the doors, there was no one there and the doors were closed.

The William III state apartments were closed the day of my visit, so I was unable to investigate this particular haunt, however, you can view the CCTV footage at:
https://youtu.be/lne_ye2UYBo.

Fountain Court's Ghosts
Fountain Court is located farthest from the main entrance. The court is bounded on all four sides by covered arcades; a large fountain occupies the center of a manicured lawn. The court is reputed to be haunted by a ghostly procession known as the Cavaliers.

As I walked the court's north arcade, I suddenly felt an excruciating pain in my left shoulder that emanated downward into my chest area. The pain was so intense that it literally made my legs buckle and I actually fell to the ground for a few moments!

I sensed the presence of a male ghost who was sharing with me his pain of death. That clue would be useful in identifying him later when I returned home and researched the history.

In the 1850s, Lady Jane Hildyard, sister of the fourth Marquess of Townshend (1817-1878), lived in the apartments adjacent to Fountain Court. Lady Hildyard complained of a ghost who knocked on the door to her quarters, and when she opened the door, no one was there.

(Photo: Hampton Court Palace, Fountain Court. Credit: R. Gutro)

The mystery of the ghostly knocking was solved when workers installing new drains in the courtyard uncovered the skeletal remains of two men killed in 1689 during construction of the new apartments. They were buried in the same courtyard where they met their untimely end.

The pain that I experienced was shared by one of the construction workers when he was crushed by falling debris.

So why didn't the construction worker cross over? Sometimes when a person dies in an accident, they awaken as energy and may be confused. Once they linger for an extended period of time, they forget to cross over and wind up trapped on Earth as a ghost. I believe that is what happened with this particular man's ghost.

The Spirit of Queen Jane Seymour

Reports of seeing Queen Jane Seymour's apparition on the Silver Stick Staircase date back as far as the 1800s. Rather than seeing her ghost, I sensed the presence of her spirit. I'll explain in a moment. But first, let's recap Queen Jane's story.

Just a mere 11 days after the execution of Queen Anne Boleyn, Henry VIII married Lady Jane Seymour (his third wife) on May 30, 1536. On October 12, 1537, Jane retired to Hampton Court, a customary ritual of the day, where she gave birth to a boy. Just 12 days later, Jane died of puerperal fever in her royal apartments.

The queen's apartments from Jane's time no longer exist, but the Silver Stick Staircase that once accessed the floor to the rooms survives. Each year, on October 12, the anniversary of her son's birth, Queen Jane's visage has been seen ascending the stairway in a white gown carrying a candle. Her apparition has also been sighted in Clock Court on the same date.

Now my explanation for why I think that Jane's apparition is a spirit and not a ghost. Earthbound ghosts usually linger in a fixed location and can appear at any time of the year whenever there is energy present to give power to manifest themselves. Spirits, however, like those of our loved ones, have crossed over and appear only on special dates – birthdays, anniversaries, and holidays. Since Jane's

(Photo: Hampton Court Palace, Fountain Court. Credit: R. Gutro)

The mystery of the ghostly knocking was solved when workers installing new drains in the courtyard uncovered the skeletal remains of two men killed in 1689 during construction of the new apartments. They were buried in the same courtyard where they met their untimely end.

The pain that I experienced was shared by one of the construction workers when he was crushed by falling debris.

So why didn't the construction worker cross over? Sometimes when a person dies in an accident, they awaken as energy and may be confused. Once they linger for an extended period of time, they forget to cross over and wind up trapped on Earth as a ghost. I believe that is what happened with this particular man's ghost.

The Spirit of Queen Jane Seymour

Reports of seeing Queen Jane Seymour's apparition on the Silver Stick Staircase date back as far as the 1800s. Rather than seeing her ghost, I sensed the presence of her spirit. I'll explain in a moment. But first, let's recap Queen Jane's story.

Just a mere 11 days after the execution of Queen Anne Boleyn, Henry VIII married Lady Jane Seymour (his third wife) on May 30, 1536. On October 12, 1537, Jane retired to Hampton Court, a customary ritual of the day, where she gave birth to a boy. Just 12 days later, Jane died of puerperal fever in her royal apartments.

The queen's apartments from Jane's time no longer exist, but the Silver Stick Staircase that once accessed the floor to the rooms survives. Each year, on October 12, the anniversary of her son's birth, Queen Jane's visage has been seen ascending the stairway in a white gown carrying a candle. Her apparition has also been sighted in Clock Court on the same date.

Now my explanation for why I think that Jane's apparition is a spirit and not a ghost. Earthbound ghosts usually linger in a fixed location and can appear at any time of the year whenever there is energy present to give power to manifest themselves. Spirits, however, like those of our loved ones, have crossed over and appear only on special dates – birthdays, anniversaries, and holidays. Since Jane's appearances are connected to a specific day, her apparition is more likely a spirit.

(Photo: Hampton Court Palace, Silver Stick Staircase. Credit: R. Gutro)

On my visit, I did not sense any paranormal activity in the area of the stair; in fact, it was a dead area without an energy signature. At first, I thought that was odd, given the number of reported sightings of Jane Seymour's ghost. But that meant, very simply, that Jane's spirit was not around. This made sense to me, because spirits don't linger; they return to the energy of the cosmos and only return when to recognize something that is meaningful for them.

The Hidden Door
The royal apartments once occupied by Henry VIII no longer exist.

(Photo: Image of an orb above Stewart's head.
Credit: R. Gutro)

Over the years, the palace has seen many renovations, and the king's apartments were completely gutted and renovated in the 17th century. It was in this area that I met a docent named Stewart who shared his own paranormal experience. He also showed us one very cool thing that most people don't get to see.

Although Henry VIII's apartments no longer exist, there is one remnant that has survived: a secret door that once opened onto a stair that connected the king and queen's bedchambers. Stewart pulled back the curtain to reveal the door; it was very exciting to touch a piece of history.

I was so in awe of the door, that I didn't sense the ghostly visitor standing with us. It wasn't until I was writing this book and reviewing the photos taken that day, that I saw an orb floating above Stewart's head. A ghost had been present with us in that small room.

Stewart's Personal Ghost Story
I related to Stewart that I have the ability to sense ghosts and spirits. I asked him if he believed in ghosts, and if he had had an encounter that he'd like to share. Stewart was only too happy to oblige. He prefaced his story by stating that he had never believed in ghosts until his encounter at Hampton Court.

He escorted us into a series of rooms known as Queen Caroline's private apartments and told me that was where he had seen a ghost. Stewart said "On the day of my encounter I was reviewing my script, thinking about what I was going to say to people."

As visitors began filtering into the room, Stewart said he began a conversation with a woman seated in the window. He said, "Suddenly I saw this movement out of the corner of his eye.   A figure, more like a silhouette, went speeding off (he made the motion of running with his arms swinging) through the window, went off, goodness knows to where!"

 "It was literally over in seconds and I got the impression of a silhouette, quite tall," he said. "It was a bit strange for a moment. Wherever it had gone to, it was gone."

Ghosts can appear as dark silhouettes if they don't have sufficient energy to manifest themselves as a full figure.

For Stewart's video story, go to:
https://youtu.be/7ZXF6lppGJ0

Residual Energy in the Kitchens
Along the northern edge of the palace is Carpenter's Court. This internal street is where the kitchens are located. The kitchens, built in the 1530s, were in continuous use until 1737, and one of the best surviving examples of a working kitchen from the Tudor period. The meals for as many as 400 guests, twice a day, were prepared here.

As I entered the first kitchen, I immediately felt intense residual energy, triggered by the presence of my own emotional energy. Also present was the residual odor of food preparation. Not only was it amazing to get such an olfactory sensation from energy, but it also smelled good.

Great Gate House Ghost Walks Through Me
Queen Catherine wasn't the only ghost that walked through me at Hampton Court; a ghostly guard did the same thing as we departed the palace grounds.

(Photo: Great Gate House. Credit: R. Gutro)

As we walked under the imposing arch of the Great Gate House, my entire body suddenly became chilled. I realized a ghostly guard walked through me, continuing his watch hundreds of years after his death. He was pacing back and forth, and I just happened to cross his path.

The reason living people experience chills when a ghost passes through them is because the ghost absorbs some of the living person's body heat. Ghosts need energy from the living to manifest themselves. So, when I crossed the ghostly soldier's path, he took some of my body heat and left me chilled.

The Ghost in the Garden
Hampton Court Palace has an extensive network of elegant gardens that cover over 60 acres. It was no surprise that one of the gardeners from centuries ago prefers to spend their afterlife there.

(Photo: Hampton Court Palace, Garden Statue. Credit: R. Gutro)

The gardens are filled with statuary and fountains. There are over one million flowering bulbs. The yew trees are beautifully sculpted into triangular shapes. There's also a maze consisting of a half mile of winding paths, created as a humorous diversion for the court of William and Mary.

In the formal garden located on the east side of the palace, I encountered the ghost of a gentle gardener, still absorbed in his work. He gave me the impression that he worked in the gardens during the 1540s and was content to continue tending the gardens that he loved, and seems to be enjoying the activity that he has chosen to do for eternity.

Hampton Court Palace had more ghosts than any other place I visited in England. Some of them were famous, like Queen Catherine Howard, while others were not so famous, like the gentle gardener.

Meeting such a diverse group of ghosts was a reminder that people stay behind as earthbound ghosts for a myriad of reasons. Whether linked to a terrible tragedy or to happiness, they all made a choice to stay behind, trapped as an earthbound ghost. Even if they stay behind for positive reasons, ghosts really don't belong on this earthly plane, forever separated from their loved ones in spirit who have already crossed over.

One of the highlights of my visit to Hampton Court was my encounter with the docent Stewart, who kindly shared his own ghostly experience.

If you visit Hampton Court, be sure to keep an open mind. As you walk through the rooms and courtyards where I had experiences, you may have a few of your own.

PART 4:

ENCOUNTERS WITH MANY GHOSTS OF THE TOWER OF LONDON

Chapter 16:
Tower of London Ghosts and Portal

The Tower of London is a castle located on the north bank of the Thames River. Originally constructed by William the Conqueror in 1066, the castle is best known for being a prison, but it also served for a long time as a royal palace. The castle is comprised of a complex of buildings surrounded by a double wall and moat. The most prominent building is the old keep, called the White Tower, with its four towers capped by Tudor domes.

During the Tudor period, the Tower's use as a royal residence began to decline and its use as a place to safeguard royal offenders began to take off. Some of them were executed on the castle's Tower Green and still linger as earthbound ghosts.

According to the book *Haunted London* by Rupert Matthews, there are quite a number of ghosts in the Tower, including a grey lady, a man wearing fifteenth century clothing, a lady in white, the audible screams of Guy Fawkes, a male ghost in the Bell Tour, ghostly knights, and more.

*(Photo: Tower of London, Exterior.
Credit: R. Gutro)*

Weather is a Contributing Factor

On the day of my visit, the weather made the Tower even more ominous. The skies were overcast, and intermittent showers made the day especially chilly and dreary. Whenever there's a low pressure system, accompanied by rain and lightning, it all adds energy to the atmosphere, energy used by ghosts to manifest themselves. So, the setting was primed for ghostly activity.

Chapel Royal of St. Peter ad Vincula

St. Peter ad Vincula is a small chapel located within the walls of the tower. The chapel fronts onto Tower Green, the site of many of the castle's executions. The remains of all prisoners executed within the castle's walls have been interred within the chapel.

*(Credit: St. Peter ad Vincula, Exterior.
Credit: R. Gutro)*

A partial list of names of those buried in the chapel includes two of Henry VIII's wives – Queen Anne Boleyn and Queen Catherine Howard, Lady Jane Grey and her husband, Guildford Dudley, George Boleyn and his wife, Jane, Thomas More, Thomas Cromwell, and Edward Seymour, brother of Queen Jane Seymour.

The Ghost of Anne Boleyn Communicates
Prior to taking the tour of the chapel, I had no pre-existing knowledge on the historical significance of the church, nor who might be interred beneath the floor. As I entered the chapel, there was a great sense of foreboding and grief present in the atmosphere. The docent requested that everyone

take seats in the chapel's pews. As I did so, my feelings of anxiety and grief swelled, and I became emotional to the point of tears. I sensed the presence of a female energy sharing their feelings with me.

The docent began to tell the story of Anne Boleyn, and how her ghost has been seen in the chapel. At this point, I realized that it was Anne's ghost who had been sharing those emotions with me.

According to *Guide to Castles of Europe*, the most persistent ghost in The Tower of London is the ghost of Queen Anne Boleyn. Anne's ghost is said to appear near the Queen's House, close to the site of her execution. Some people have said her ghost has been seen leading a procession down the aisle of the Chapel.

Ghosts will often share their pain of death, or the emotional feelings they were experiencing at the time of their death. Anne chose to share the latter with me.

The Ghost of Sir Walter Raleigh
Sir Walter Raleigh was an explorer and courtier; he was a court favorite of Queen Elizabeth I. As a reward for his military victories, he was knighted in 1585. There is some speculation that there may have been a romantic attachment between the queen and Raleigh, which explains why she had him arrested and thrown in the tower for secretly marrying one of the queen's ladies-in-waiting, Elizabeth

Throckmorton. But the queen quickly forgave the couple, and Raleigh was released from the tower.

Raleigh led several expeditions to the New World. He is credited for introducing tobacco and potatoes to England.

While on an expedition to South America in 1616, Raleigh was implicated in the raid of a Spanish outpost, a violation of the terms and conditions of a peace treaty with Spain. When Raleigh returned to England, he was arrested and executed.

(Photo: Tower of London, Sir Walter Raleigh's Room. Credit: R. Gutro)

The rooms occupied by Raleigh are still furnished as they were in the 16th century. His ghost has been seen in the vicinity, pacing the floor.

Ghosts of the Two Princes

Two ghosts who are reputed to haunt the Bloody Tower are just boys. The two boys are believed to be the young sons of Edward IV – Edward and Richard. When the king died in 1483, the oldest of the boys, Edward, became king, and their uncle was appointed Lord Protector. Under the guise of taking the boys into protective custody until the coronation, they suddenly vanished and were never seen again. Their uncle usurped the throne and became King Richard III.

In 1674, workmen found the skeletal remains of two children beneath a stone staircase. The remains were put in an urn, and re-interred in the Henry VII Chapel in Westminster Abbey.

To this day, the mystery as to what happened to the two young princes has not been solved, but the ghosts of two small boys seen haunting the Bloody Tower may very well be the two missing princes.

Ghostly Soldier Outside

Just before entering the White Tower, I saw the figure of a soldier walking down the stone path between the buildings. At first sight, I thought he was a living person in period costume because he was wearing a uniform consistent with the 1600s. Moments later, he vanished as quickly as he appeared so I realized he was a ghost.

(Photo: Tower of London, Location of the encounter with a ghostly soldier. Credit: R. Gutro)

It's very rare that I will see a full-bodied, full-color apparition, but he appeared and looked like a living, breathing person wearing a period costume.

I was unable to get any information from him and he was too far away to determine if he was residual energy or an intelligent haunt. I suspect that if he was a residual haunt, the apparition would march over and over, traversing the same spot.

My Shocking Experience at Salt Tower

Salt Tower was once known as "Baliol's Tower" because of its famous prisoner, John Baliol, King of

Scotland, who was imprisoned there from 1297 to 1299.

Throughout the Tower, prisoners left behind graffiti carved in the stone walls of their cells. Hugh Draper of Bristol, carved an intricate, astronomical clock. Jesuit priests carved religious scenes. But the most intriguing paranormal experience occurred at the Salt Tower's entry.

As I opened the door, and stepped through the opening, I heard a loud audible buzzing sound, accompanied by a pulsing sound wave.

The doorway is most likely a portal, a way for earthbound ghosts to travel to and from two different points. Portals do not connect to a location in the light, they only connect to places in the Earth plane of existence.

As paranormal investigators, Tom and I immediately attempted to debunk the experienced. We checked the room and the wall surfaces around the doorway for sources of electrical current, exposed wiring, or audio-visual devices that could produce a sound wave. Finding none of these, we concluded the experience must have been paranormal.

Once through the doorway, the room fell silent. The room was filled with a sense of stillness and emptiness.

(Photo: Tower of London, Location of the encounter with a ghostly soldier. Credit: R. Gutro)

It's very rare that I will see a full-bodied, full-color apparition, but he appeared and looked like a living, breathing person wearing a period costume.

I was unable to get any information from him and he was too far away to determine if he was residual energy or an intelligent haunt. I suspect that if he was a residual haunt, the apparition would march over and over, traversing the same spot.

My Shocking Experience at Salt Tower
Salt Tower was once known as "Baliol's Tower" because of its famous prisoner, John Baliol, King of

Scotland, who was imprisoned there from 1297 to 1299.

Throughout the Tower, prisoners left behind graffiti carved in the stone walls of their cells. Hugh Draper of Bristol, carved an intricate, astronomical clock. Jesuit priests carved religious scenes. But the most intriguing paranormal experience occurred at the Salt Tower's entry.

As I opened the door, and stepped through the opening, I heard a loud audible buzzing sound, accompanied by a pulsing sound wave.

The doorway is most likely a portal, a way for earthbound ghosts to travel to and from two different points. Portals do not connect to a location in the light, they only connect to places in the Earth plane of existence.

As paranormal investigators, Tom and I immediately attempted to debunk the experienced. We checked the room and the wall surfaces around the doorway for sources of electrical current, exposed wiring, or audio-visual devices that could produce a sound wave. Finding none of these, we concluded the experience must have been paranormal.

Once through the doorway, the room fell silent. The room was filled with a sense of stillness and emptiness.

Having time to reflect back on the experience, I have now concluded that whatever ghost or ghosts haunt Salt Tower are using the portal to go to another part of the castle. When I opened the door, I happened to have walked into the portal just as it was closing.

(Photo: Tower of London, Doorway to the Salt Tower. Credit: R. Gutro)

It's important to note that living people can't be transported through the portal, only beings of energy can, like ghosts. Living people can only feel the pulsating energy of a portal.

The Ghosts of Salt Tower

Salt Tower is one of the most haunted areas of the Tower.

Paranormal groups that have investigated the Tower and brought dogs to identify the presence of paranormal activity. The dogs would not even enter Salt Tower because they can see and hear the ghosts.

(Photo: Tower of London, Window in the Salt Tower. Credit: R. Gutro)

Dogs have a different physiology in their eyes and they can hear at higher frequencies than humans. Ghosts move at a higher vibration than human eyes can see, but dogs can see that faster movement. Ghosts have been known to speak at higher or lower frequencies than humans can hear, which is why paranormal investigators use digital recorders to capture those sounds.

In 1864, a soldier guarding the Queen's House saw an apparition that looked like a living, breathing person. The soldier's report indicated he thought the person was an intruder, so the soldier charged at the intruder with his bayonet. The weapon went right through the apparition.

There are many reports of other ghosts seen in Salt Tower: ghosts of Jesuit priests, Lady Jane Grey and Guildford Dudley. Lady Jane Grey's ghost was last seen by two guards on February 12, 1957, on the 403rd anniversary of her execution. The guards described her as a "white shape forming itself on the battlements."

The ghost of Lady Jane's husband, Guildford Dudley, has also been seen weeping in Beauchamp Tower.

Emotional Energy at Traitor's Gate
Prisoners brought to the tower by boat entered the castle by way of Traitor's Gate, often passing the decomposing severed heads of previous offenders mounted on pikes.

Historical accounts document that Queen Anne Boleyn and Queen Catherine Howard both passed through Traitor's Gate. Catherine Howard, in all likelihood, would have observed the heads of her paramours Thomas Culpepper and Francis Dereham.

It is not difficult to imagine the feelings of anxiety and fear experienced by prisoners; their residual emotional energy imprinted on the stones surrounding the gate area. This energy can be easily felt by living people who are sensitive.

(Photo: Tower of London, Traitor's Gate.
Credit: R. Gutro)

Final Thoughts
The Tower of London was filled with the emotional energy and the ghosts of former occupants. The emotional energy consisted fear, anxiety,

nervousness, anger, and depression. All of these emotions emanated from prisoners once held here, and were absorbed by its stone walls.

My most unique paranormal experience was the portal in Salt Tower. It was my first time experiencing the physical sensation of such a phenomenon. However, I was not successful in locating the other associated portal that serves as the end point for the Salt Tower portal.

Both historically fascinating and tragic at the same time, mediums and sensitives are bound to have an experience there.

PART 5:
MY GHOSTLY
ENCOUNTERS
OUTSIDE OF LONDON

Chapter 17:
The Ghosts of Canterbury

Canterbury is an English cathedral city located in Kent. Its name is derived from the old English word "Cantwareburh" meaning "Kent people's stronghold."

*(Photo: Canterbury War Memorial.
Credit: R. Gutro)*

There are many popular tourist destinations in the area including the Roman Museum, the ruins of St. Augustine's Abbey, the Dane John Mound, and the ruins of Canterbury Castle. But it's the Cathedral, the site of a most unpleasant grisly murder of a monk that is probably why the town is so well known in the paranormal community. Of course, the town is more famous from Geoffrey Chaucer's book, *The Canterbury Tales*.

The Haunted Magic Shop
The Pure Magick Shoppe, located on St. Peters Street, is purported to have three ghosts. So of course, I had to investigate this potential hotspot of ghostly activity.

As soon as I entered the shop I immediately sensed the ghost of a woman. She seemed benign and welcoming. However, I was unable to confirm who she was or why she was there.

When in a public place, it becomes difficult for a medium to concentrate and focus on the entity when there is a lot of activity from the living present; their added energy is often the source of interference. That's why on paranormal investigations, it has been my experience that the more successful investigations have been those where the number of investigators has been kept small, limiting the amount of emotional energy and creating less interference for communicating with ghosts.

Since I was unable to focus on the energy of the female ghost, I went upstairs to see if I could connect with some of the other ghosts reputed to haunt the shop. It was there that I encountered the energy of a male ghost who was not as welcoming as the female ghost on the first floor.

As I attempted to telepathically communicate with the male ghost, he physically turned away from me, an indication that he wanted me to leave. I complied with his request.

Ghosts maintain the same personalities in death as they had in life. The male ghost has obviously been very anti-social in life, and the woman on the first floor was a much more sociable and agreeable person in life. My next step was to learn who they were, why they were there, and determine if they wanted help crossing over.

(Photo: The Haunted Pure Magick Shoppe. Credit: R. Gutro)

I returned to the first floor and asked the shop owner and his female co-worker about the hauntings. Normally, I would have been more cautious about engaging in such a conversation, but since this was a magic shop and there were a number of paranormal items being offered for sale, I felt more comfortable about the situation.

They confirmed the presence of the male ghost upstairs and said he has been seen wearing a long black overcoat and sometimes a hat. The ghost has been seen walking through the wall into the adjoining retail shop next door. To me, this is an indication that the magic shop and the adjoining establishment had once been one undivided structure, most likely a house. Usually when a ghost is seen walking through a wall, there was in all probability a door in that location when the person lived in the physical world.

The shopkeepers told me of a more recent encounter with the male ghost by a customer. The customer went upstairs and immediately came back downstairs after a very brief period. The customer told shop owner that there was something upstairs that didn't want him there. The story of this encounter was identical to what I had experienced, so I will take that as a confirmation of the ghost's personality. Obviously, he doesn't want anyone disturbing him.

The shopkeepers, both sensitives, confirmed the presence of the female ghost on the first floor. The woman had lived and worked in that very store when it was a dress shop in the 1950s. She is reported to be short in stature, wears her hair up, and is a very smart dresser. Although the name of the female ghost remains a mystery, it is apparent that she is content.

One More Ghost

Although I did not encounter the third ghost, the shopkeepers had met her and had this story to tell.

The ghost is that of a little girl who is spending her afterlife in the shop. The ghostly girl likes to tug on customers' clothing, and giggle loudly. She walks around in the shop and doesn't seem to be restricted to just one floor. So, if you visit the magic shop, and feel a gentle tugging on your jacket, it may very well be the ghost of the giggling little girl.

The Ghost of Thomas Becket

Canterbury Cathedral is called the "Mother Church of the Anglican Communion" and is the seat of the Archbishop of Canterbury. The Cathedral is a UNESCO World Heritage Site, and its history extends as far back as 597 A.D. when St. Augustine was sent to Britain as a missionary and he established the first church in Canterbury. The Cathedral is famous for being the site of Archbishop Thomas Becket's grisly murder by four knights. Since then, the Cathedral has been both a pilgrimage destination and tourist attraction.

Less than 100 years after William the Conqueror, England's central government had become totally dysfunctional because of feuding between its power-lusting lords and barons. Matilda, daughter of Henry I, was unable to keep her claim on the throne and subsequently was usurped by her cousin, Stephen. Matilda's son, Henry, barely 20 years old at the time, raised an army and returned from Normandy to reclaim the throne by force. Exhibiting his military prowess, Henry successfully brought the barons to heel, reunited the kingdom, and was crowned King Henry II.

(Photo: Canterbury Cathedral, Exterior. Credit: R. Gutro)

Thomas Becket was the son of a merchant. While still a young man, he went to work for the Archbishop of Canterbury, and quickly rose up through the Church's hierarchy by proving himself to be an excellent administrator. Becket gained influence with the king by resolving conflicts between the Church and Henry, often to the king's advantage. Henry and Thomas became quick friends and drinking buddies, and in spite of their age difference, they often hunted together and enjoyed rousing debates. But Henry had a fiery temper, which eventually caught up with him.

When the Archbishop of Canterbury died in 1162, Henry bullied the council of bishops into electing his friend, Thomas, to be the next archbishop.

Once installed, Becket turned his back on the king, and became very pious. To even the score with the new archbishop, the king presided over a ceremony officially recognizing his son as heir and the next king and excluded the archbishop. To this day, this anointing ceremony of the monarch is totally the Archbishop of Canterbury's gig, and when Thomas learned what the king had done, he excommunicated all who were involved. The story goes that Henry flew into a rage, and said, "Will no one rid me of this meddling priest?" Taking the retort as a directive, four knights looked for Becket and killed him as he was offering up prayers inside the Cathedral.

Becket's body was interred beneath the floor in the Cathedral's east end. In 1220, his remains were relocated to a shrine in Trinity Chapel. During the dissolution of the monasteries under Henry VIII, the shrine and Becket's remains were destroyed. Today a stone paver in the floor, engraved with "Thomas," marks the location inside the Cathedral where the murder occurred. Both the Catholic and Anglican Churches have venerated Becket as a saint and martyr.

(Photo: Stone marker locating where the murder of Thomas Becket occurred. Credit: R. Gutro)

As I was standing near the marker, I sensed the presence of a male energy. Suddenly, the ghost told me he was Thomas Becket.

As a medium I am able to sense aspects of someone's personality, and I found Becket to be very headstrong and stubborn. It was then I began to understand how there could have been conflict between Becket and the king.

Chapter 18:
The Ghosts of Stratford-Upon-Avon

Located on the River Avon, Stratford-Upon-Avon is best known as the birthplace of William Shakespeare. The town's original charter was granted in 1196, making Stratford over 800 years old. The house where Shakespeare was born, the home of Shakespeare's daughter, a tavern that he was known to frequent, and the church where Shakespeare is buried all survive to this day.

The Ghosts of Old Thatch Tavern
The Old Thatch Tavern is located on Greenhill Street. The tavern is a traditional English pub that has been in business since 1623, and is the only thatched roof building in the whole town. If you visit, be sure to try the fish and chips; they were fantastic.

The tavern's menu actually recounts a story about the ghost who haunts the tavern. A man named James Pinfield was being chased by a group of Irishmen; he ran inside the tavern to hide. The men found him and dragged him back outside the tavern where they murdered him. To this day, James Pinfield's ghost is said to still haunt the pub.

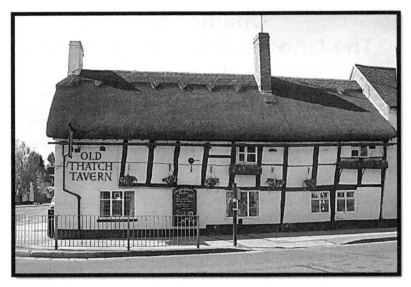

(Photo: Old Thatch Tavern, Stratford upon Avon. Credit: R. Gutro)

The Ghostly Server

While enjoying dinner, I saw a woman walking around the restaurant, serving people. I noticed that she was wearing clothing from another period, like the 1600s or 1700s. I thought that was odd because the other serving staff were dressed in contemporary attire. Although I could see her, it took me a couple of minutes to realize that she was a ghost.

Concentrating on her energy, I asked for her name. She told me her name was Emily and pronounced it "Emi-lee." She had brown hair, pinned up and covered by a white bonnet; the bonnet was tied around the bottom with a black ribbon.

Emily wore a white dress covered by a dark-colored vestment. She was carrying a basket with several loaves of bread, and a red napkin covering the top of the basket.

She seemed to linger and walk around in the back of the tavern. In fact, she lingered there so long that I had time to draw a sketch of her.

(Photo: Sketch of the ghost of Emily.
Credit: R. Gutro)

Shortly after I finished the sketch, a crowd entered the tavern. It was then that I realized my characteristic ghost headache had gone away, and when I looked up, so had Emily's ghost.

The Energetic Cemetery
Cemeteries are not usually haunted. Ghosts typically haunt places that they frequented in life or perhaps

the location where they died. At the Stratford-upon-Avon Cemetery located on Evesham Road, there were no intelligent haunts, but there was a lot of residual energy. That energy was so strong that it gave me a clue about what claimed many of those buried there.

Upon entering the cemetery I immediately sensed that energy. Most of it was emanating from children who were interred there. I sensed that a significant number of them had died from the flu, measles, or chicken pox.

(Photo: Stratford-upon-Avon Cemetery. Credit: R. Gutro)

Those feelings were confirmed as I walked further into the cemetery, and noticed all of the grave markers for children ranging in age from just a few months to 10 years of age. The magnitude of the amount of residual energy I was sensing indicated to me just how large a number of the children were buried there.

I did not sense any intelligent haunts or interactive ghosts in the cemetery, which was not surprising. It was all totally residual energy.

Although it is unusual to feel a lot of paranormal activity in a cemetery, if you're sensitive to energy you'll likely feel the residual energy in this one.

A Ghostly Couple in Hall's Croft
Hall's Croft is the name of the home owned by Shakespeare's daughter Susanna and her husband, Dr. John Hall. The structure is an excellent example of an original half-timber building from the 1600s.

Located outside the house is a garden filled with herbs that Dr. Hall most likely would have used in the preparation of his medicinal remedies.

As I entered the first floor I developed my characteristic ghost headache, followed immediately by chest pain which indicated to me someone had passed from a heart-related issue. These feelings also indicated that I was dealing with an intelligent haunt, or interactive ghost, because residual energy is unable to share past physical pain. At the onset of pain, John told me that he was the male ghost standing next to me.

It was only once I started touring the house that I learned that Susanna's husband was named John. Of course, then was able to make the connection that this was the ghost who was talking to me. I learned that John died in 1635, at the age of 60 years; the cause of death most likely being a heart attack – which confirmed the sensations I experienced when I walked through the front door.

Oh, Susanna!
While sitting on a bench in the garden, my headache returned, almost as if the ghost of John had followed me outside. But I soon realized this was not the case. This time it was Susanna who was outside in the garden with me.

The story these two entities shared about their current situation is that after John passed, he stayed behind to help others. When Susanna passed, she sensed that her husband's energy was earthbound and chose to stay with him in the afterlife. Although John's ghost prefers to spend his afterlife inside the house, Susanna's ghost seems to thoroughly enjoy being outside in the garden.

More information about ghost sightings in Stratford-Upon-Avon can be found at:
https://www.stratfordtownwalk.co.uk/

Chapter 19:
The Ghost at Sudeley Castle

Sudeley Castle was the estate of Queen Katherine Parr, the last surviving wife of Henry VIII. There is one reputed ghost who haunts the castle, and there's a very strange story about her burial that would explain why she's not at peace.

(Photo: Sudeley Castle, Exterior. Credit: R. Gutro)

The current structure we see today was built in 1442 on top of the remains of an earlier 12th century castle by Ralph Boteler, Baron Sudeley. In addition to the castle, Boteler also built servants quarters, state and family apartments, a moat, chapel, and tithe barn. Surviving records indicate that Boteler got into some legal trouble for failing to obtain royal permission to crenellate the castle, for which he had to appeal to the king for a pardon. From this point onward, ownership of Sudeley was constantly changing.

In 1469, Edward IV confiscated the estate from Boteler, and gave it to his brother, Richard, Duke of Gloucester (the future Richard III). Richard added the Banqueting Hall and adjoining staterooms – the ruins of which are still standing. When Richard was killed in the Battle of Bosworth Field in 1485, the estate passed to the new king, Henry VII, who gave it to his uncle, Jasper Tudor.

(Photo: Banqueting Hall Ruins, Sudeley Castle.
Credit: R. Gutro)

When Jasper died, ownership of the estate reverted back to Henry VIII. When Henry VIII died, the castle passed to Edward VI, who gave it to his uncle, Thomas Seymour, along with the title of Lord Sudeley. Seymour then married the dowager queen of Henry VIII, Katherine Parr, within the prerequisite mourning period, which raised quite a few eyebrows at court.

Within a year, Katherine became pregnant and retired to Sudeley to have the child. On August 30, 1548, Katherine gave birth to a girl, Mary, but died of puerperal fever just five days later.

Thomas ended up getting into all sorts of trouble, but it was his involvement in a foiled attempt to kidnap the young King Edward that finally did him in. Seymour was arrested, convicted of treason, and executed leaving the young Mary an orphan. What happened to the baby Mary is a mystery to this day.

Katherine Parr's ghost is reputed to haunt the castle, but very little of the castle is open to the public, and I was unable to sense the presence of her energy in the areas the public is allowed to tour.

Queen Katherine's Forgotten Burial Place
On the estate is the Chapel of St. Mary. Queen Katherine Parr is buried inside the chapel just to the left of the altar. On the wall, is an engraving in Old English that reads, "Here Lyeth the queen Kateryn, Wife to Kyng Henry VIII, And Last the wife of Thomas Lord of Sudeley and High Admiral of England and Unkle to King Edward VI, Dyed 5 September." Today, the tomb is beautiful, but it wasn't always in that condition.

In 1649, Prince Rupert of the Rhine, with an army of 4,000 men, advanced on the neighboring town of Cirencester, which caused the Roundheads camped at Sudeley to flee. The Roundheads caused considerable damage to the chapel where Katherine was interred.

(Photo: Tomb of Katherine Parr, St. Mary's Chapel. Credit: R. Gutro)

The castle was abandoned, and fell into severe neglect and disrepair as locals began using the castle as a source for building materials. In 1782, a farmer wandering around on the estate stumbled into the chapel, broke into Katherine Parr's tomb, and looked inside the lead casket. Katherine's body was in perfect condition and intact. However, exposure to air turned the corpse to rapidly decompose. In 1817, a new tomb was constructed and Katherine's remains were re-interred there.

In 1837, Sudeley was purchased by wealthy glove-makers, brothers John and William Dent. In 1855, the estate passed to their nephew who opened a small portion of the castle and grounds to the public.

The Ghosts at Sudeley
Katherine's ghost can be seen wandering through the castle's corridors – the figure of a tall woman, wearing a green dress, and the faint odor of apple-scented perfume. There have also been reports of hearing the ghost of a crying child in the area of the nursery.

Why Does Queen Katherine Haunt the Castle?
There are a number of explanations for why Queen Katherine haunts Sudeley Castle.

First, she may have stayed behind to help her daughter. People remain behind as an earthbound ghost sometimes do so with the best of intentions such as helping someone. Ironically, Katherine could have done much more for her daughter if only she had crossed over and became a spirit.

Second, Katherine and Thomas' daughter, Mary, has disappeared from the historical record. Some historians propose that Mary died while still an infant, and since it was customary not to record the vital statics of female children, this would help explain why there is no account of what happened to her. Perhaps Katherine is wanting to reconnect with her lost child. Since Mary is long dead, if she crossed into the light, Katherine cannot communicate with her as earthbound ghosts are unable to communicate with spirits.

Finally, the desecration and destruction of her tomb in the 17th century could be another reason why her ghost remains restless in the castle. Whatever the reason, she'll be there for eternity unless someone can cross her over.

Chapter 20:
The Mary Rose Museum Energies

The Mary Rose Museum, located in the dockyards of Portsmouth, contains the remains of Henry VIII's flagship, which sank in 1545 when the ship took on too much water through its open gun ports. The ship's remains were discovered in 1971, and recovered from the seabed in 1982. In addition to the remains of the ship, the museum contains salvaged artifacts and forensic reconstructions of the ship's crew based on their recovered skeletal remains.

(Photo: Artillery salvaged from the Mary Rose. Credit: R. Gutro)

Sensing Intense Energy
As a medium, walking through a museum with artifacts is very much a similar experience as walking through an antiques shop. The sensations I receive

can be overwhelming because I feel the emotional energy that people have left on the items.

As I walked through the museum, I was feeling the energy emanating from the imprint of the men that served on the ship. I also picked up on an intense feeling of dread – imprinted in the structure of the ship during the crew's realization that the ship was sinking.

About the *Mary Rose*
The Mary Rose is a carrack-type (masted) warship. It was named for Henry VIII's daughter, Mary, and the Tudor family's symbol - the rose. Built in 1510, it was the flagship of King Henry VIII's royal navy; she sank in the Solent (the body of water separating the Isle of Wight from mainland England) during a battle with a French invasion fleet. During a tactical maneuver, the ship attempted to turn around. Wind caught the sails, and caused the ship to list too far. The ship took on water through the open gun ports and sank. Some historical accounts state that Henry watched the battle from the shore and witnessed the ship's sinking.

When the Mary Rose sank, half of the ship was submerged in the sand and muck on the bottom of the seabed; this portion of the ship was preserved while the exposed half eroded away.

Once raised out of the ocean, because the ship's remains had been submerged for so long, exposure to air would hasten its deterioration.

So conservation efforts included pumping resin under extreme pressure, into the cells of the wood fibers essentially plasticizing the remains.

*(Photo: Image of the conservation effort.
Credit: R. Gutro)*

Artifacts recovered from the ship's salvage operations include artillery, cannon, pottery, utensils, personal effects belonging to the crew, and the crew's skeletal remains including "Hatch," the ship's dog.

Forensic scientists conducted DNA testing on some of the crew's remains. There's a fascinating exhibit where forensic artists have reconstructed the faces and bodies of some of the crew, and even identified the mixed breeds of the dog. Of course, being a dog dad, Hatch's story was of particular interest to me. One item that I was especially drawn to was a brick with an impression of what is believed to be Hatch's paw. Apparently, Hatch walked through the moist clay of the formed brick before it had been fired.

The museum is definitely a must-see attraction. As a medium, the emotional energy attached to so many of the items on display was at times overwhelming. There were no ghosts in the museum; the crew that passed when the ship sank have all crossed over.

PART 6:

OUR HAUNTED CASTLE ROOM

Chapter 21:
Solving the Ghostly Mystery at Thornbury Castle

Construction of Thornbury Castle began in 1511, by Edward Stafford, of the Plantagenet family. Edward was the son of Henry Stafford and Katherine Woodville, whose sister was Queen Elizabeth Woodville, wife of Edward IV.

Stafford believed that his claim to the throne was more legitimate than that of the Tudors, which was tenuous at best. For this reason, King Henry VIII viewed the Plantagenets as a very real threat. Mounting evidence suggested that Stafford was indeed covertly plotting and scheming behind the king's back, and he was arrested, tried for treason, and executed on May 17, 1521.

(Photo: Thornbury Castle, Exterior.
Credit: R. Gutro)

At his death construction on the castle stopped and ownership of his estates reverted to the crown. The majority of the castle remains unfinished.

Today the castle is a luxury hotel. A significant part of the original 16th century structure and gardens has survived. There is amazing detail in everything from the ornate ceilings to the original oriel windows with their leaded glass panes.

For more information about the castle and its accommodations, visit:
http://www.thornburycastle.co.uk/

*(Photo: Thornbury Castle, Exterior.
Credit: R. Gutro)*

Henry VIII Slept Here
Henry VIII and Anne Boleyn stayed at the castle while on their progress in 1535; the bedchambers they occupied still exist.

The Unfinished Parts

What appears to be ruins are actually the parts of the castle that remain unfinished from when the construction was discontinued in 1521. Walking in these areas, I did not detect any paranormal activity.

The Famous Ghost in Our Room

When a ghost finds a living person who can sense their presence, they often try to communicate with them. That's what happened during our overnight stay at Thornbury Castle.

Our room was located at the top of a winding staircase in one of the castle's towers. Instead of a room number, there was a sign on the large wooden door with the room's name. Upon entering the room, I immediately developed my characteristic ghost headache. A ghost had followed us into the room.

After checking out the room we decided to walk into town for dinner. We left the room and stopped in the entryway just outside the suite door to pose for pictures while holding the giant skeleton key to the door. When Tom took my picture, there were no anomalies. But when I took his picture, an orb appeared above his head.

After taking the pictures, I sensed that the ghost walked back through the door and returned to the room. We decided that we would deal with the ghost when we returned from dinner.

(Photo: An orb appears at the door of the suite as Tom poses for a picture. Credit: R. Gutro)

Gathering Clues to the Ghost's Identity

When we returned to the room after dinner, my headache also returned, indicating that our paranormal guest was still in the room.

We took several pictures with the digital camera to see if we could locate the ghost, but were unsuccessful. Analysis of the images later revealed the presence of an orb; and the orb hovered in front of the curtains near the room's only window.

We decided to unwind and try and get answers from the ghost the next day. I took a shower and got ready for bed; that water energy was exactly what the ghost needed to give me a clue to his identity.

Moving water contains a lot of energy so the ghost tapped into that energy to help identify himself. While in the shower, I heard the name "Rupert." The ghost revealed to me his name.

(Photo: Image of an orb. Credit: R. Gutro)

The next thing Rupert said to me was "Wittenham." Being unfamiliar with the area and its history, the name meant nothing to me at the time.

A Request for Ghostly Quiet

How do you get a good night's sleep when there's a ghost in your room? You make your request nicely, with respect, as if you were communicating with a living person. So, I asked Rupert if he would kindly go downstairs while we slept. Before turning in, the lock on the door and latch on the window were both checked and found to be secure.

(Photo: Thornbury Castle, image of the bed in the room where we stayed.
Credit: www.tripadvisor.co.uk)

Ghost Conveys Sleeping Conditions

It was a very restless night with very little sleep afforded to either of us. By all outward appearances, the bed appeared to be very comfortable, but during the night, it felt as if there was a wooden divider beam lengthwise down the center of the bed, and in lieu of a mattress, the bed felt as if it had been stuffed with hay.

When we checked the bed the next morning, it felt soft and comfortable and totally unlike what we experienced while trying to sleep.

I later realized that Rupert was conveying the sleeping conditions he often experienced when he was alive. I didn't know that ghosts could do something like that. I figure that since ghosts can share pain, scents and other things, it makes sense that Rupert could share that sensation.

Rupert's Grand Entrance
At 5:30 a.m., just as the sun was peeking over the horizon, the window flew open and slammed against the stone wall of the castle, waking both of us out of a sound sleep.

I got up out of bed, walked over to the window, and looked outside. There was no wind, so that was immediately ruled out as a cause. The latch of the iron window grate was on the inside, and the room was located on the third floor, so the window had to be released by someone standing inside the room! Once again, my ghost headache returned, and I realized that Rupert's ghost was responsible for opening the window.

Wittenham
The word "Wittenham" nagged at me. I didn't know if it was the name of a town, another castle, or a person. My research revealed that "Little Wittenham" is a village located on the River Thames in South Oxfordshire, about 86 miles east of Thornbury Castle. That distance makes it believable that Rupert could have visited that location and Thornbury when he was alive.

The Rupert and Wittenham Connection
In an out-of-print book entitled, *"Letter Books 1644-1645, Sir Samuel Luke,"* I found the following reference to Rupert: "It is reported that *Prince Rupert*

is marching with all his forces towards Oxford, and that Lord Digby is made Chief. He was carried prisoner from Reading on Saturday morning with the king's forces to *Little Wittenham."* Now I knew that Rupert was a prince.

Uncovering Rupert's Story
I spent a lot of time trying to find Rupert's connection to Thornbury Castle. My research revealed that Prince Rupert was born in 1619, and had been a Royalist military commander during the English Civil War.

At the siege of Bristol, on September 10, 1645, Rupert surrendered to Lord Fairfax. Bristol is located just 12 miles from Thornbury Castle. He was court-martialed and acquitted of all charges. He was dismissed from service in 1645 by King Charles I. Rupert later founded the scientific Royal Society.

Although he never married, he had a daughter named Ruperta by his mistress Peg Hughes. He died in 1682 and is buried in Westminster Abbey.

Now that I knew his life history, the next mystery was figuring out why he was haunting Thornbury Castle.

The Rupert and Thornbury Connection
It's always a challenge to determine why someone has decided to remain earthbound as a ghost and why they choose to haunt a certain location.

Based on my post-vacation research, my best guess about Rupert's connection to Thornbury Castle is because it's one of the last surviving structures in that area from the period of the English Civil War.

(Photo: Thornbury Castle, Exterior. Credit: R. Gutro)

Why Did Rupert Stay Earthbound?

Since Rupert didn't offer an answer to why he stayed behind as an earthbound ghost I had to rely on history to find a reason.

Not only was Rupert's surrender at Bristol a big blow to his military career, but I believe it was perhaps *the* biggest disappointment of his life, a setback from which he never fully recovered emotionally. So Rupert chose to linger in an area within close proximity to the site of that battle, reliving it over and over, and hoping to change the outcome.

PART 7:
A FRIEND'S SPIRIT
PROVIDES VACATION
HELP

Chapter 22:
Timely Help from a Spirit

Although this book is about the ghosts I encountered on my travels in England, this story is about the spirit of Tom's late friend Ed. Ed appeared in the form of a living, breathing man who resembled him. That man helped us out of a bad situation.

Spirits cross into the light and can travel anywhere at any time. They watch over us, wherever we go, and help us when needed. Fortunately, Ed's spirit was there when we needed him.

Tom and Ed were best of friends in the late 1980s and 1990s. Ed passed from an unexpected accident in 1996 and although I never knew him in life, through my relationship with Tom, Ed's spirit has appeared to me many times. So, I feel as though he's a close friend that just happens to live in another place. In my book *Lessons Learned from Talking to the Dead,* I wrote about how Ed's spirit took us on a "spirit treasure hunt."

This adventure began when our guidance system malfunctioned for some odd reason. I would later figure out that perhaps there was a reason...

GPS Unit Goes Haywire
When we picked up our vacation rental car, we also rented a GPS unit for navigation purposes.

As we departed Bath we typed the address of our next destination into the GPS. We had been driving for approximately one hour when the GPS directed us to take the next exit. Since the GPS had been accurate for hours, there was no reason to suspect that something was amiss. We took the exit and left the highway, soon finding ourselves driving on a two lane road.

Twenty minutes later, the two lane road turned into a narrow country lane, with twists and turns. When the GPS told us to veer off the narrow lane onto a dirt road with grass growing in the center, we knew that something was not right. We backed out of the dirt road, and onto the lane, totally lost, and unable to figure out how to return to the highway.

Tom attempted to reprogram the GPS, while I parked and got out of the car to search for a living person to ask directions. Anxiety was mounting because it was late in the afternoon and the sun had already dropped below the tree line.

The Arrival of Ed's Doppelganger
After sitting on the shoulder of the lane for about five minutes, a Royal Mail truck came up over the hill behind us. I flagged down the driver and he pulled over.

The driver who stepped out of the truck was about my height, with a slender build and a mop of black hair flecked with grey. His face was thin, and he wore glasses. As I explained our predicament to the driver,

I thought this stranger looked very familiar. The mailman said that after he made the three remaining deliveries on that street, he would show us the way back to the highway. I thanked him and returned to the car.

*(Photo: Image of Ed around 1992.
Credit: Tom W.)*

As I got into the car, Tom said, "He looks just like I imagine Ed would look today." He continued, "If you recall the photos of Ed, just give him gray hair and glasses, and that's what our rescuer looks like." I agreed. I had seen enough photos of Ed to know that it very well could have been him.

We followed the mail truck being driven by Ed's doppelganger for several miles and as we approached the exit to the highway, he waved us off in the direction we needed to go. As he drove off in the opposite direction, I marveled at how spirits work. I truly feel as if I finally met Ed in person for the first time, after all these years.

The more I thought about that chance encounter with the Royal Mailman, I realized that Ed had just responded to long held desire of mine: a wish to meet him in person. So Ed made it happen.

Because spirits and ghosts are energy, they have the ability to manipulate electronics, like a GPS unit. It's likely that Ed caused the GPS to malfunction on purpose, knowing that his look-alike would be driving a mail truck down that road five minutes after we stopped.

Obviously he can't come back in person, so he created the opportunity for me to meet someone that strongly resembled him.

Spirits can do amazing things. Now...what's with changing up that southern drawl with a British accent?

PART 8:
THE GHOSTS OF WINDSOR

Chapter 23:
Ghosts of Windsor

The city of Windsor is famous for Windsor Castle, the Crooked House, and Eton College, but I will remember it for my two encounters with the same ghost over two years.

The "Holy Ghost" of Holy Trinity Church
The one place in Windsor where I encountered an intelligent haunt was the Holy Trinity Church. The ghost attached to the church connected with me on two separate trips taken in two successive years.

In 2012, as I walked past the building, I suddenly developed my characteristic headache. As I walked around the perimeter of the structure, my investigation led me to the front doors. It was there that I saw the figure of a ghostly vicar, wearing vestments, standing on the front steps, directing his congregants inside.

I also saw apparitions of former parishioners who were all residual energy. They were an amalgamation of the figures of people, collected over time, repeating the same action of entering the church where they once worshipped. They were residual haunts.

The vicar, however, was an intelligent haunt. I telepathically asked his name; and he replied, "Desmond." He also gave me the date of "1850" to help identify him. I bid Desmond a good day and he acknowledged me as we parted.

I later learned that the church was built in 1842, dedicated to the soldiers that served under Queen Victoria.

(Photo: Holy Trinity Church, Windsor. Credit: R. Gutro)

As for why Vicar Desmond remains earthbound, I offer the simple explanation that he continues to enjoy doing the very same activity in the afterlife that he once enjoyed in life.

A Second Encounter
When I returned to Windsor the following year, the ghost of Vicar Desmond was still happily greeting his "parishioners." Seeing the vicar again proves that ghosts have the ability to make a choice. Vicar Desmond will apparently stick around for a very long

time, welcoming the residual energies of his long-dead parishioners as well as the new, living parishioners. Or the occasional passersby.

Windsor Castle Ghosts
The tour of Windsor Castle is restricted to less than a dozen rooms. As I toured the castle, I could sense a tremendous amount of residual energy, but I did not encounter an interactive ghost.

The castle and grounds are reputedly haunted by the ghosts of Queen Elizabeth I, George III, and Henry VIII.

Elizabeth I's ghost has been seen wearing a black dress, standing at a window in the Dean's Cloister. She has also been heard walking in the Royal Library.

George III was one of England's longest-reigning monarchs. When he died on January 29, 1820, he was blind, deaf, and mad. His remains were interred in St. George's Chapel. His ghost has also been seen standing in one of the castle's windows.

Before George III died, however, he is said to have encountered the ghost of Queen Elizabeth I. The "Mad King" claimed to have had a conversation with a woman wearing black who then suddenly vanished.

The remains of Henry VIII are buried in the vault located below the choir in St. George's Chapel. Henry's groaning ghost can be heard making the sound of dragging his ulcerated leg behind him.

It has been my experience that ghosts tend to haunt places that they loved in life, rather than where their remains may have been interred. For this reason, I suspect that the ghost haunting the chapel is more likely to be that of a monk or religious person, rather than Henry VIII. Henry is more likely to be haunting one of his palaces. On my visit, St. George's Chapel felt peaceful and devoid of any paranormal activity.

PART 9:
THE GHOSTS OF YORK

Chapter 24:
The Ghosts of York

The City of York is best known for its village-like retail area called the Shambles, Clifford's Tower, and its monumental cathedral called York Minster. In addition to being the birthplace of Guy Fawkes, it is also the home to a few ghosts. On my visit, I encountered both residual energy throughout the city, and an interactive ghost while enjoying a meal at one of the local establishments.

The Ghosts in York Minster
The site where York Minster stands today has been continuously occupied since the time of the Romans back in 71 A.D.

In the basement of the cathedral is a fascinating exhibit that recounts the origins story of York; also on display are the foundations of an ancient Roman fort, the ruins of the original Roman settlement, as well as coins and other artifacts unearthed during the archaeological digs on the site.

The first structure built on the site for religious purposes was constructed in 627, to baptize King Edwin of Northumbria. By 637, a stone edifice replaced the original wooden one. Over the centuries, there have been many church buildings on the site; construction of the present building began around 1220 and was completed in 1472.

As with any church, there is usually a heavy thumbprint of emotional energy that is absorbed by the structure. York Minster was no different.

(Photo: York Minster, Exterior.
Credit: R. Gutro)

People have been coming to this particular site for over a 1,000 years, and left their energies behind – feelings include hope, despair, desires, destitution, optimism, peace, anxiety, depression, and happiness; emotions that span the entire spectrum of human experience, like a heavy blanket to anyone who is sensitive to them.

On my visit, I just knew that there had to be plenty of ghosts sitting in the pews right beside the living people. One such ghost is that of Dean Gale, who died in 1702 at the age of 26; he's been seen sitting at the end of one of the pews, still listening to sermons.

The Ghost at Bootham Bar

York is a medieval walled city, and there are four main gates in the wall, called 'bars.' The four bars are Bootham Bar, Monk Bar, Walmgate Bar, and Micklegate Bar.

Although much of what we see today of Bootham Bar was built in the 14th and 19th centuries, it also has some of the oldest surviving stonework in York dating back to the 11th century.

As I passed through the gate, I could sense a tremendous amount of residual energy attached to it, but no intelligent haunts, not even a ghostly guard was anywhere to be found. There is, however, the story that the ghost of a nun has been seen wandering around in the vicinity of Bootham Bar. If there is a ghostly nun attached to the gate, she was likely off praying somewhere when I visited.

The Ghost at the Lamb and Lion Inn

There's nothing like having an uninvited guest drop in during dinner. That's what happened when dining with friends at the Lamb and Lion Inn, located right next to Bootham Bar.

(Photo: The Lion and Lamb Inn.
Credit: R. Gutro)

When I entered, I immediately sensed the presence of a male energy. He was very excited that I could sense him, and told me that he had owned a shop located on the same site where the inn is today. He was definitely an intelligent haunt and could interact with me.

In life, he had been very dedicated to his work, and loved his vocation. When I inquired as to why he was there, he told me that he was still waiting for his wife. However, I sensed that when the wife passed, she immediately crossed over. I told him that and hope that he has crossed over and rejoined her.

Clifford's Tower

Clifford's Tower, originally the castle keep, is the remnant of a Norman fortification that once occupied this ancient Roman mound. What remains today is the stone structure built by Henry III in 1245.

*(Photo: Clifford's Tower, York.
Credit: R. Gutro)*

In 1190, the small Jewish community of York sought protection from an anti-Semitic mob inside the wooden keep. The unruly mob stormed the castle, and lit the structure on fire. Many of the 150 Jews holed up in the keep committed suicide, while others died at the hands of the rioters.

The entire area surrounding the stone tower gives mediums and sensitives a very heavy feeling. Standing outside the tower at the bottom of the mound, I sensed the fear, anguish, and panic of the people who died there more than 800 years before. Those emotions have left a very sad emotional thumbprint on the land.

Local legend says the tower turns red in color from the blood of all the people who have died at that location.

The Shambles

Anyone who visits York has to spend time in the Shambles. The narrow lanes, and timber-framed buildings overhanging the streets, complete the quaint Old World atmosphere. I had no personal encounters in this area, but there is guaranteed to be a lot of living energy on any day you visit.

(Photo: The Shambles, York. Credit: R. Gutro)

One of the ghosts who has walked the streets of the Shambles for over 100 years is that of a tall, well-dressed gentlemen wearing a bowler hat. The last time he was seen was during World War II. I didn't encounter the tall ghostly stranger, but because the streets were so crowded with tourists on the day of my visit, he could have walked right by me. It was difficult to see every living person, let alone try to spot the dead ones

A weathered plaque affixed to the wall of one of the shops provided a history of the famous district. The plaque read, "The ancient street of the Butchers of York mentioned in the Domesday Book of William the Conqueror. It takes its name from the word 'Shamel,' meaning the stalls or benches on which the meat was displayed - later versions of which can still be seen. It was rebuilt around 1400 when it assumed its present character."

The Shambles is an amazing place to visit, from a retail, historic, and architectural perspective. Don't miss it.

PART 10:
MY MOST AMAZING PARANORMAL EXPERIENCE IN ENGLAND

Chapter 25:
The Ghost Guide at Hever Castle

My visit to Hever Castle will forever be imprinted on my mind because of the very special ghost who accompanied me. My ghostly guide was persistent and one of the most communicative ghosts I have ever encountered. Unfortunately, taking pictures inside the castle was not allowed. If I could have taken pictures, I'm sure that I would have captured an image of his orb.

Hever Castle is located in the picturesque village of Hever, Kent, about 30 miles southeast of London. The castle was built in the 13th century, and from 1462 to 1539, it was the home of the Boleyn family.

*(Photo: Hever Castle, Exterior.
Credit: R. Gutro)*

Sir Thomas Boleyn, father of Queen Anne, inherited the castle in 1505 and immediately began renovating it to meet the needs of his growing family; a significant amount of what was done to the castle during this time has survived. After the death of Thomas in 1539, ownership of the castle reverted back to Henry VIII. In 1540, the estate was given to Anne of Cleves, Henry's fourth wife, as part of their divorce settlement.

Over the years, the property passed through various owners, and fell into serious disrepair until it was eventually purchased by the American millionaire William Waldorf Astor in 1903. Astor spared no expense in the castle's restoration, with historical accuracy being very important. The castle gardens, designed by well-known gardeners of the time Joseph Cheal & Son, were implemented between 1904 and 1908. In 1983, the castle was sold to a property management company which runs the estate as a conference center, but the castle and grounds are open to the public.

Being a dog dad myself, I was extremely moved by the pet cemetery. The Astors had an extreme fondness for dogs as well. Each grave was marked by a headstone engraved with the name of their beloved pet.

First Encounter with the Ghost
Upon entering the castle, I instantly developed my characteristic headache that lets me know when a ghost is present. Then I heard a male voice say, "I'm George." I had no idea who George could be, so I asked Tom who informed me that "George" was the

name of Anne's brother. So now I knew to whom I was talking.

Ghosts often haunt places that they enjoyed in life, or places where they died. George's ghost chose to reside in his boyhood home of Hever.

Once George greeted me at the front door I didn't expect him to follow me through the castle. When he realized I could hear him, he wanted make sure that I heard everything he had to say – a typical response from ghosts when they discover that a living person possesses the ability to sense their presence.

Introduction to George Boleyn
George rode the coattails of his family's rising fortunes because of Anne's influence with the king. In 1525, he was made Gentleman of the Privy Chamber; in spite of what the duties of this title entailed, it was a highly regarded position. In 1529, he was knighted and granted the title Lord Rochford.

George was accused of incest with his sister, Anne. He was put on trial and in spite of his very eloquent defense, was convicted of high treason. On May 17, 1536, he was beheaded on Tower Hill.

George's Pride
As we continued to walk and talk (telepathically), George's love for his sister, Anne, really came through to me. He told me that he was "very proud of her." The last thing George said to me was the year "1532." He said that that was a time in his life when

he was the happiest. At the time, I was unaware of the significance of the date.

(*Photo: Sketch of George Boleyn.
Credit: R. Gutro*)

name of Anne's brother. So now I knew to whom I was talking.

Ghosts often haunt places that they enjoyed in life, or places where they died. George's ghost chose to reside in his boyhood home of Hever.

Once George greeted me at the front door I didn't expect him to follow me through the castle. When he realized I could hear him, he wanted make sure that I heard everything he had to say – a typical response from ghosts when they discover that a living person possesses the ability to sense their presence.

Introduction to George Boleyn
George rode the coattails of his family's rising fortunes because of Anne's influence with the king. In 1525, he was made Gentleman of the Privy Chamber; in spite of what the duties of this title entailed, it was a highly regarded position. In 1529, he was knighted and granted the title Lord Rochford.

George was accused of incest with his sister, Anne. He was put on trial and in spite of his very eloquent defense, was convicted of high treason. On May 17, 1536, he was beheaded on Tower Hill.

George's Pride
As we continued to walk and talk (telepathically), George's love for his sister, Anne, really came through to me. He told me that he was "very proud of her." The last thing George said to me was the year "1532." He said that that was a time in his life when

he was the happiest. At the time, I was unaware of the significance of the date.

(*Photo: Sketch of George Boleyn.*
Credit: R. Gutro)

When I returned home, my research revealed that on September 1, 1532, the king bestowed on Anne the title of the Marquess of Pembroke. With this title, she became a royal. No wonder he was proud of her.

George in the Dining Room

The dining room is one of parts of the castle that survive from the time of the Boleyn family; it was one of the additions to the castle built by Thomas in 1506, along with the "Long Gallery" immediately above it. It was in this very room that the family would have dined with Henry VIII.

When I entered the dining room, I got a pain in my left elbow. George's ghost pointed to the ornate fireplace and said, "I was burned as a boy near the fireplace in this room." Of course, there's no record of George burning his elbow, so I just have to believe what he told me.

George's Biggest Regret

George biggest regret centered on his time spent at the court of Henry VIII. He told me, "I should never have gone to court." He was foolish to have ever trusted the king, knowing Henry's past. He told me that had if he had chosen to avoid the life of a courtier, he could have lived such a full life. Instead, his life was cut short so tragically and at such a young age.

What George Wanted

George was insistent he was innocent of the charge of having sexual relations with his sister. George said that Henry feared that George would try to kill him, so he made up a lie to remove the threat of George along with his sister. George wanted confirmation that others know the truth, so that he can cross over and be at peace.

I acknowledged George's feelings and thanked him for sharing his words, experiences, and feelings with me. I told him that people today know about Henry's paranoia, and how the king manipulated people and lied about them to get them out of his way.

We walked through the remainder of the castle without any other messages from George, and I realized that he finally heard the answer he's been longing for - that he was at peace knowing that had been framed.

Chapter 26:
When You Visit

Now that you've read about the encounters that I had in England, I hope that you will be inspired to visit. The paranormal is just an added bonus to all the rich history, culture, and people. When you go, here are some things to keep in mind:

Highlights
1) Henry VIII's Hampton Court Palace - Truly a highlight of my visits. It was here that I encountered the screaming ghost of Catherine Howard on two separate occasions. Also a great place to see a concert. I was fortunate enough to see Sir Cliff Richard perform there.
https://www.hrp.org.uk/hampton-court-palace/

2) Hever Castle and Gardens – Home of the Boleyn family, and later gifted to Queen Anne of Cleves, Henry VIII's fourth wife. It was here where I encountered the ghost of George Boleyn. The gardens on the property are spectacular.
https://www.hevercastle.co.uk/

3) Sudeley Castle and Gardens - Home of Queen Katherine Parr, Henry VIII's sixth wife. As with Hever Castle, the gardens were beautiful.
https://www.sudeleycastle.co.uk/

4) The Mary Rose Museum, Portsmouth - This new museum is dedicated to conserving the remains of Henry VIII's flagship – the Mary Rose, which sank in 1545. After almost 500 years underwater and mired in

the seabed of the Solvent, it was recovered in 1982, brought to the surface, and a museum built around it. The museum contains artifacts salvaged from the wreckage, as well as forensic reconstructions of the ship's crew. It first opened to the public in 2013.
www.maryrose.org/

Before You Go
Here are some tips to help you plan your travel, should you decide to visit these haunted places.

5) Trains - Trains are a great way to see the country. One thing we learned was that train tickets may also be used for one connection on the Tube (subway) in London.

6) Flights - Heathrow is a huge airport. If you're using Heathrow to connect with other flights, allow a minimum of 2 hours to clear customs and security screening.

7) Weather in England – Expect that it will rain. For forecasts and average temperature information, visit the UK Meteorological Service website:
http://www.metoffice.gov.uk/

8) Driving - Driving on the left side of the road can be a bit of a challenge. If you rent a car in London you will get a fast lesson. Always get a GPS unit. Although sometimes our GPS didn't work, it was still a helpful tool. It's also a good idea have a paper map, too.

9) Street Width – Streets are much narrower than they are in the U.S. and the widths are not always consistent. I was glad that we rented a compact car.

In rural areas, roads are narrower than in the city; they twist and turn like crazy. Expect to wait for oncoming traffic to pass as the roads are often too narrow for two vehicles to pass simultaneously, particularly in villages.

10) Speed Limit Signs and Measurements - Speed limits are in miles per hour, *not* kilometers per hour. What's interesting is that all other measurements are in Metric. Most locals seem to drive about 60 mph, even on the narrow, twisting country roads. I drove about 35 mph so as to avoid scraping the vegetation or stone walls that line the roads.

11) Coffee or Tea? - Drink tea. I am a huge coffee drinker, but the coffee served in the U.K. is either instant or Dark French Roast - two choices I don't care for. I learned to really enjoy hot tea. Iced tea is not served in eating establishments, but you can get it in most convenience stores.

12) English Food - English food is not that bad. Of course, I'm a plain eater. Give me a burger and fries, or fish and chips, and I'm set. So long as there's a cookie or cake afterward. There are a lot of bakeries, which was great.

13) Lodging in Windsor – When in Windsor, check out Langdon House Bed and Breakfast. Run by Paul and Sonja Fogg, the rooms are comfortable and a full English breakfast is served each morning. Windsor is a wonderful little city. It is pedestrian friendly, and accessible by train. For more information: www.langtonhouse.co.uk/

14) Trip Planning - Don't stress over trip planning. I recommend consulting with Across the Pond Vacations at www.atpvacations.com/. Anne Marie Clarke will put together an all-inclusive vacation package, complete with detailed itinerary, accommodations, tours, tickets, subway passes, and car rental.

Everyone should have the opportunity to visit the British Isles. If you are interested in the paranormal, there are ghosts everywhere. If you are interested in history, it's the place to visit. I hope you have found these encounters and tips helpful, and inspirational.

About the Author

(Photo: Rob at Tower Bridge. Credit: Tom W.)

Rob considers himself an average guy, who just happens to be able to hear, feel, sense and communicate with Earth-bound ghosts and spirits who have passed on.

He is a medium and paranormal investigator on the Inspired Ghost Tracking team in Maryland, U.S.

When not communicating with the dead, Rob communicates with the living. He's a meteorologist by trade who enjoys talking about weather. He speaks at schools, museums, and social organizations about weather. Rob worked as a radio broadcast meteorologist at the Weather Channel. He has almost 20 years of on-air radio broadcasting experience.

Rob is an avid dog lover who, with his husband, volunteers with Dachshund and Weimaraner dog rescues. Together, they've fostered and transported many dogs, assessing the dogs at shelters for the rescues, working with coordinators, vets, and shelters to save the lives of dogs.

Rob enjoys taking ghost walks in various cities and visiting historic houses and sites to see who is still lingering behind and encourages them to move into the light to find peace.

He still reads and collects comic books and has always loved the mysterious heroes. Since he was a boy, one of his favorite superheroes has always been the ghostly avenger created in the 1940s called "The Spectre."

Website/Blog: www.robgutro.com or
www.petspirits.com or
 http://ghostsandspiritsinsights.blogspot.com/
Facebook pages:
https://www.facebook.com/RobGutroAuthorMedium
https://www.facebook.com/ghostsandspirits.insightsfromamedium
Twitter: https://twitter.com/GhostMediumBook
Amazon Author Page: amazon.com/author/robgutro

YouTube: https://plus.google.com/collection/ok7wh
Email: Rgutro@gmail.com
Rob's Books are available in paperback and E-Book on www.Amazon.com.
They include:
Ghosts of England on a Medium's Vacation
Pets and the Afterlife
Pets and the Afterlife 2
Lessons Learned from Talking to the Dead
Ghosts and Spirits

Bibliography

CHAPTER 4
English-Heritage.org, Jewel Tower.
http://www.english-heritage.org.uk/visit/places/jewel-tower/
House of Lords,
https://en.wikipedia.org/wiki/House_of_Lords

CHAPTER 5
Westminster-Abbey Website: Queen Elizabeth I, Mary Queen of Scots, Anne of Cleves;
www.Westminster-Abbey.org
The Middle Ages.net: Richard the Lionheart, www.themiddleages.net
Ghost-Story.Co.UK: Ghost of a Benedictine Monk called "Father Benedictus," www.Ghost-Story.co.uk

CHAPTER 7
St. Paul's Cathedral, U.K. www.stpauls.co.uk.
Morton Report, the ghost in St. Paul's Cathedral, www.Mortonreport.com

CHAPTER 8
The Journal of Mrs. Soane's Dog Fanny, by Herself and Mirabel Cecil, 2010, by John Soanes Museum.
Sir John Soane's Museum Website, www.soane.org:

CHAPTER 9
Historic Royal Palaces' website: www.hrp.org.uk

CHAPTER 11
The Royal Hospital of St. Bartholomew website, www.bartshealth.nhs.uk

Haunted London, Viaduct Pub:
www.haunted-london.com

CHAPTER 12
Find a Grave.com, St. Mary's Church:
www.Findagrave.com

CHAPTER 13
Pewterers' Hall website: www.pewterers.org.uk

CHAPTER 14
Folklore Thursday, Church of Saint Bartholomew the Great: http://folklorethursday.com/regional-folklore/fools-church-rahere-church-st-bartholomew/#sthash.vEjTSB1K.dpbs

CHAPTER 15
Hampton Court Palace official website,
http://www.hrp.org.uk/HamptonCourtPalace/
Is the Palace Haunted? Palace Phantoms, brochure, Historical Royal Palaces: Hampton Court Palace's publication
Stewart the docent, 2012 video interview by Rob Gutro. https://youtu.be/7ZXF6lppGJ0

CHAPTER 16
The Anne Boleyn Files.com at:
https://www.theanneboleynfiles.com/anne-boleyns-remains-the-exhumation-of-anne-boleyn/
Haunted London, Rupert Matthews, Pitkin Publishing, Andover, Hampshire, U.K.
History-UK.com: The Princes in the Tower by Ben Johnson
http://www.historic-uk.com/HistoryUK/HistoryofEngland/The-Princes-in-the-Tower/

Castles.me.UK now Ancientfortresses.org:
http://www.castles.me.uk/salt-tower.htm
http://www.castles.me.uk/traitors-gate.htm,
Guide to Castles of Europe: http://www.guide-to-castles-of-europe.com/tower-of-london-ghosts.html

CHAPTER 17
Wikipedia.com:
https://en.wikipedia.org/wiki/Canterbury

CHAPTER 18
Visit Stratford-upon-Avon website:
http://www.visitstratforduponavon.co.uk
Shakespeare's Birthplace: www.shakespeare.org.uk

CHAPTER 19
University of Leicester, Press Release: University of Leicester announces discovery of King Richard III, Feb. 4, 2013.
http://www2.le.ac.uk/offices/press/press-releases/2013/february/university-of-leicester-announces-discovery-of-king-richard-iii
Sudeley Castle website: www.sudeleycastle.co.uk.
Haunted Britain http://www.haunted-britain.com/sudeley-castle.htm

CHAPTER 21
Across the Pond Vacations www.atpvacations.com
Britannica.com
https://www.britannica.com/biography/Edward-Stafford-3rd-Duke-of-Buckingham
Thornbury Castle www.thornburycastle.co.uk
Thornbury Castle Bedroom photo:
www.tripadvisor.co.uk
"Letter Books 1644-1645, Sir Samuel Luke," (Out of print): http://tinyurl.com/yah932zk

History Learning Site.co.Uk (17 Mar 2015. 16 Aug 2016): http://www.historylearningsite.co.uk/stuart-england/prince-rupert/
Wikipedia, "The Siege of Bristol (1645)," https://en.wikipedia.org/wiki/Siege_of_Bristol_(1645)
Wikipedia, "Prince Rupert" https://en.wikipedia.org/wiki/Prince_Rupert_of_the_R hine

CHAPTER 23
Real-British-Ghosts.com:http://www.real-british-ghosts.com/windsor-castle-ghosts.html
History.com: King George III: http://www.history.com/topics/british-history/george-iii
Haunted Island UK, http://www.hauntedisland.co.uk/famous-hauntings/ghosts-of-windsor-castle-berkshire

CHAPTER 24
Wikipedia: York Minster: https://en.wikipedia.org/wiki/York_Minster
York Minster.org: https://yorkminster.org
Haunted Rooms U.K.: https://www.hauntedrooms.co.uk/top-8-haunted-places-york-ghosts-york
History of York.org.uk: http://www.historyofyork.org.uk/themes/norman/the-1190-massacre
Yorkmix.com, Ghost in Shambles: https://www.yorkmix.com/life/history/haunted-york-some-more-of-the-citys-spookiest-ghost-stories/

CHAPTER 25
BBC UK History: http://www.bbc.co.uk/history/people/anne_boleyn/

On the Tudor Trail, George Boleyn:
http://onthetudortrail.com/Blog/resources/biographies/
george-boleyn/
Stamford Stone Company:
http://www.stamfordstone.co.uk/stone/block-stone/

57947620R00119

Made in the USA
Middletown, DE
03 August 2019